New Testament Epistles

by Heath Rogers

Published by:
One Stone Press
979 Lovers Lane
Bowling Green, KY 42103

Printed in the United States of America

ISBN: 978-1-941422-64-9

www.onestone.com

Table of Contents

Dedication

This book is dedicated to my friend and mentor, Mike Pittman.

Introduction

What is an epistle? Simply put, an epistle is a letter. These letters were the means the apostles and other writers used to communicate God's will to Christians when they could not do so in person (1 Corinthians 14:37; Ephesians 3:3-4). The epistles were also written to remind and encourage Christians to remain faithful to the Lord (Hebrews 13:22; 2 Peter 1:12-15; 1 John 2:12-14).

When we approach the gospels (Matthew, Mark, Luke and John), we know we are going to learn about the life of Jesus. The book of Acts contains the history of the establishment of the church and the initial spread of the gospel. However, the 21 epistles in the New Testament vary in their content. Some are written to local churches; some are written to individuals; and some are written to Christians at large. Some are easy to read and understand, while others deal with complex doctrinal matters. Many of them combine "meaty" doctrine with practical application.

This workbook is a survey of the New Testament epistles. The lessons consider the reason each epistle was written, summarize its contents, and highlight important truths that we can use in our daily lives.

I am extremely grateful to Carolyn Bixby for taking the time to proofread this material. Many of her suggestions are a part of this workbook.

Unless otherwise noted, all Bible quotations are from the New King James Version.

Lesson 1

Romans

Highlights

The gospel is God's power to save mankind (1:16).

All have sinned and fallen short of God's righteousness (3:23).

The wages of sin is death, but the gift of God is eternal life in Christ Jesus (6:23).

We are more than conquerors through Him who loved us (8:37).

Do not be conformed to the world, but be transformed by the renewing of your minds (12:2).

Author

Paul authored this epistle.

Date

57-58 AD

Romans is one of the few epistles that can be dated with a good degree of certainty. Paul wrote it at Corinth while he was on his third missionary journey. Paul was traveling to Jerusalem with the collection made by the churches of Macedonia and Achaia (compare Acts 20:2-4 and Romans 15:25-28). His travel took him to Corinth, where he stayed three months. During this time, Paul wrote Romans.

Purpose

To help Jewish and Gentile Christians find unity in Christ.

Spotlight

The gospel is God's power to save both Jews and Gentiles.

For I am not **ashamed** of the **gospel** of Christ, for it is the **power** of God to **salvation** for everyone who **believes**, for the **Jew** first and also for the **Greek**.

- Romans 1:16

We are not exactly sure how the church in Rome was established, but it is evident that no apostles had been there (Romans 1:9-11). As with many first-century churches, the church in Rome was made up of Jews and Gentiles. This letter specifically addresses each group.

Jews and Gentiles had lived separately both socially and religiously for centuries. Bringing them together into one body through Christ was God's eternal plan, but it had its challenges. Paul wrote this letter to explain how God, who is no respecter of persons (Romans 2:11), can use the same gospel message to save both Jew and Gentile, and how those who are saved are to live, work, and worship together in the local church.

And this continued for two years, so that **all** who dwelt in **Asia** heard the **word** of the Lord Jesus, both **Jews** and **Greeks**.

- Acts 19:10

Also, Paul made no secret of his desire to visit the church in Rome and to use such a visit as an opportunity to further the gospel (Romans 15:20-24). Paul was an evangelist. He sought for the most effective ways to spread the gospel far and wide. Earlier on his third missionary journey, he stayed in Ephesus for two years, and as a result of his efforts, "all who dwelt in Asia heard the word" (Acts 19:10).

Paul may have written this epistle as a means of paving the way for his personal visit to Rome. The gospel could easily and effectively be carried from this city throughout the Roman Empire. To accomplish this task, the church needed to be equipped with a solid understanding of God's scheme of redemption.

God's Scheme of Redemption (Chapters 1-8)

Paul begins the epistle by establishing his identity as an apostle and expressing his desire to visit the church in Rome (1:1-15). He sets forth as the subject of his epistle the gospel being God's power to save everyone who believes (1:16) and proceeds to establish the universal need for this salvation.

The Gentiles had turned away from a knowledge of God, descending into idolatry and immorality (1:18-32). The Jews reading this letter would have given this a hearty "Amen!" but Paul proceeded to show that the Jews were also guilty of sin (chapter 2). They had God's law but failed to keep it.

Chapter 3 concludes that both Jew and Gentile are under sin and stand condemned before God (3:23). Salvation is available, but man cannot find it in the works of the Law of Moses. Man is justified freely by God's grace through the redemption He has made available in Christ Jesus (3:24). The word *justified* means to be declared innocent. God does not ignore or overlook our sins. His law requires punishment, and Jesus satisfied this requirement when He died on the cross. This allowed God to be *just* (true to Himself and His law) and the *justifier* (able to pronounce us "not guilty" with regard to our sins) of those who have faith in Jesus (3:26).

QUESTIONS

1. Why did Paul want to visit the church in Rome (1:11)? ____________________

   ____

   ____

2. Who can be saved through the gospel (1:16)? ____________________

   ____

   ____

3. Explain why the unbeliever is without excuse (1:18-20). ____________________

   ____

   ____

4. What state are all people in before God (3:9-10, 23)? ____________________

   ____

5. How is man justified (3:28)? ____________________

   ____

   ____

The Jews criticized Paul for rejecting the Law of Moses. As he continues his letter, Paul explains how justification by faith, apart from the Law of Moses, has always been a part of God's plan (chapter 4). To prove this point, Paul turns to Abraham—the father of the Jewish nation. Abraham was not considered righteous because of his perfect works but because of his incredible faith and trust in God. Salvation is not a wage earned through law keeping. Salvation is a gift of God's grace received through faith.

Chapter 5 discusses the atoning work of Jesus. Jesus made peace with God possible when He died on the cross for our sins thus being reconciled with God. To *reconcile* means to make friendly again. Our sins make us enemies of God (5:10; Isaiah 59:1-2). Jesus took away this offense and allowed us to be reunited with God. Just as Adam brought sin and death into the world, Christ made righteousness, justification, and eternal life available to all mankind.

God's grace freely saves us, but this does not mean we can be careless about sin (chapter 6). Paul gives two illustrations that can help us understand our relationship with sin. First, we are to consider ourselves dead to sin and alive to God (6:1-14). As far as our involvement in sin is concerned, we are dead—we can no longer participate. Second, we must consider ourselves set free from the bondage of sin and enslaved to God in righteousness (6:15-23). We can no longer participate in sin. We must obey our new Master.

QUESTIONS

6. Explain what makes Abraham's faith so great (4:18-21).________________

7. What does it mean to be reconciled? ________________

8. Explain how Jesus, by dying on the cross, was able to reconcile us back to God (5:8-11).________________

9. After what is baptism modeled (6:3-4)?________________

10. When does one walk in "newness of life" (6:4)? ________________

After describing the struggle we face in sin without Christ (chapter 7), Paul presents the blessings we now have in Christ (chapter 8).

QUESTIONS

11. List the blessings we now have in Christ as set forth in Romans chapter 8.

v. 1 ____________________

v. 16 ____________________

v. 18 ____________________

vv. 26-27 ____________________

v. 31 ____________________

v. 37 ____________________

vv. 38-39 ____________________

Paul's Desire for Israel (Chapters 9-11)

Much of the Bible focuses on the nation of Israel. This nation received God's great promises and His covenant law. Now that we obtain salvation through faith in Christ, it seems as if Israel has been discarded. Where does Israel now stand with God?

Israel had a track record of rejecting God, its ultimate expression in the crucifixion of His Son. God used Israel's disobedience (11:30-31) to bring about man's salvation. However, the Jews didn't lose everything. They could be saved if they came to God through faith in Christ.

QUESTIONS

12. What was Paul's desire and prayer for Israel (10:1)? ____________________

13. What two things are essential for salvation (10:9-10)? ____________________

14. What is the source of our faith (10:17)? ______________________________

____

____

15. What did Paul want the Romans to consider (11:22)?______________________

____

____

Life as a Christian (Chapters 12-16)

We now come to the practical portion of this great letter. Understanding everything God has done to bring about my salvation, how should I now live in response to this great blessing?

In chapter 12, Paul implores us to offer ourselves as living sacrifices to God (12:1-2). As members of the local church, we are to serve one another in love (12:3-21).

These Christians lived in the capital city of the Roman Empire. Many of the Emperors were wicked men, and some of them even persecuted Christians. The gospel calls upon us to submit to the governing authorities, obey the law, and pay our taxes (13:1-7). We are to love our fellowmen who are outside the church and conduct ourselves properly in the world (13:8-14).

Every Christian has a responsibility to maintain peace and unity in the local church. There can be no compromise in matters of doctrine, but peace is often threatened by our differences in matters of personal liberty and opinion. Regarding these things, Paul instructed the church members to receive and bear with one another (14:1-15:13). Instead of judging one another and insisting on having our own way, we are to seek things that build up the body of Christ and further the kingdom of God.

In closing this great letter, Paul speaks of his plans to visit them and presents greetings to and from numerous brethren (15:14-16:27).

QUESTIONS

16. What are we to present to God (12:1)? ______________________________

____

17. Identify some of our responsibilities toward our brethren (12:3-21).

____

____

____

18. Identify some of our responsibilities toward our government (13:1-7).

____

____

____

19. Explain how love fulfills the law (13:8-11). _______________

____

____

____

20. What are those who are strong in the faith to do (15:1)? _______________

____

____

____

21. What two things are to be done to those who cause divisions and offenses (16:17)? _______________

____

____

Paul wanted to visit the church in Rome but had been prevented from doing so. Instead, he wrote this letter, speaking of the gospel's power to save all mankind. It is recognized as Paul's great masterpiece, setting forth in detail God's scheme of redemption. God, who is no respecter of persons, has made Jews and Gentiles one body through His Son Jesus Christ. Members of the local church should respond to God's grace by working and worshiping together in peace, spreading the gospel to those who are lost.

Lesson 2

First Corinthians

Highlights

We are not to think beyond what is written (1 Corinthians 4:6).

The Christian's body is the temple of the Holy Spirit (1 Corinthians 6:19-20).

No temptation has overtaken you except such as is common to man (1 Corinthians 10:13).

The proper way to observe the Lord's Supper (1 Corinthians 11:23-34).

The greatest gift is love (1 Corinthians 13).

The weekly contribution (1 Corinthians 16:1-2).

Author

Paul authored this epistle.

Date

55 AD

Paul wrote First Corinthians from Ephesus during his third missionary journey (Acts 19:10).

Purpose

To help the Corinthians overcome their various problems.

First Corinthians addresses numerous problems going on in the church. Some of these problems were reported to Paul from various sources (1 Corinthians 1:11; 5:1; 11:18). Others address questions the Corinthians had sent to Paul (1 Corinthians 7:1).

Spotlight

Christians working, living and giving together.

Now I **plead** with you, brethren, by the name of our Lord Jesus Christ, that you all speak the **same thing**, and that there be no **divisions** among you, but that you be perfectly **joined together** in the **same mind** and in the **same judgment**.

- 1 Corinthians 1:10

Division in the Church (Chapters 1-4)

Division in the local church is a serious matter. This church was not on the verge of dividing—they had already divided, and this division manifested itself in various ways, many of which are addressed in this epistle. Paul addresses this problem first because it is pointless to address any of their other problems until they overcome their division.

Paul points out, to their shame, the fact that they had divided themselves into groups, identifying with their favorite preachers (1:5). These preachers were not crucified for the Corinthians; the Lord was. The gospel's power is in the message, not the messenger. The people of the world reject this gospel message as foolishness, but those who are saved recognize it as God's power and wisdom (1:18-25).

God's word is not a rival philosophy of the day. It is God's mind revealed to us by the Holy Spirit (2:6-13).

Preachers are not the focal point of the church. Christ and His gospel are. Preachers are *ministers* who plant and water (3:5-8), *builders* who labor to build on the foundation of Jesus Christ (3:9-17), and *stewards* who faithfully dispense the Lord's gospel (4:1-2). No Christian should place any person above God's word (4:6).

QUESTIONS

1. What serious problem did Paul address in this epistle's first four chapters?______________________________

2. What is the solution to this problem (1:10)?____________________

3. Who has revealed God's mind to us (2:10-12)?____________________

4. Explain why we should not put preachers on pedestals. ____________

Sin in the Church (Chapters 5)

Next, Paul addressed the fact that the church was tolerating sin in its midst. One of the members was engaged in a form of sexual immorality so disgusting that even the Gentiles found it offensive—a man had his father's wife. This woman was likely the man's stepmother.

Paul told them they should be ashamed and should mourn this situation. He commanded them to cast this person out of the church (5:4-7, 13). This action was for the purpose of bringing the sinner to repentance and keeping sin out of the church.

Lawsuits and Sexual Immorality (Chapter 6)

This congregation's division was also made evident by the members' taking one another to court. By not settling their problems among themselves, they were causing the Lord's church to look bad before unbelievers. This airing of the church's dirty laundry defeated any effectiveness they might have in trying to influence and save the unbelievers around them (6:1-7).

Instead of living righteous lives, these Christians were sinning against one another. Although they had been terrible sinners, they had turned to Christ to receive washing, sanctification and justification. Now, they appeared to be reverting to their previous ways (6:8-11).

Known for its affluence and immorality, Corinth was home to the temple of Aphrodite which was served by 1,000 priestesses (prostitutes). Throughout the Roman empire, the people used the phrase "to live like a Corinthian" to refer to the sins of drunkenness and fornication.

Apparently, some of the church members continued to visit the temple and participate in the ritual immorality offered there. Paul explained that fornication is a sin one commits against his own

And such were some of you. But you were **washed**, but you were **sanctified**, but you were **justified** in the name of the **Lord Jesus** and by the **Spirit** of our **God**.

- 1 Corinthians 6:11

body (6:12-20). The Christian is to flee from sexual immorality. Our physical bodies are not our own to do with as we desire. Our bodies belong to God, and we are to use them in ways that glorify Him.

QUESTIONS

5. What did Paul tell the church to do about the brother who was guilty of sexual immorality (5:4-7)? ______________________________

____

____

6. Identify the kinds of people who will not inherit the kingdom of God (6:9-11). ______________________________

____

____

____

7. Explain why Christians must not involve themselves in sexual sins (6:18-20)

____

____

____

Marriage and Divorce (Chapter 7)

In this chapter, Paul answers some of their questions regarding marriage and divorce. He explains that marriage is the only lawful and honorable way of fulfilling natural sexual desires (7:1-5).

Apparently, they had questions regarding what to do when a couple separated. Paul said they must either reconcile or remain unmarried (7:10-11). Christians were not to put away their spouses just because they were not Christians (7:12-16).

Paul went on to say that individuals should not marry, but he gave these instructions in light of "the present distress," which we understand to be a period of persecution and hardship the people were experiencing at that time (7:25-40).

Christian Liberties (Chapters 8-10)

The division in the church at Corinth was also seen in the way members handled their differences in matters of judgment. This city was full of idol temples, and many members had been converted from that false religion.

Some of them realized there was nothing wrong with eating meat offered to idols. Others still believed it was wrong. This caused problems in the church.

In these three chapters, Paul set forth an important principle that we still follow today. We must be willing to forgo our own liberties and rights for the sake of our brethren (8:9-13).

Paul showed how he was already following this rule by refusing to accept payment from them for preaching the gospel (9:1-18). He was willing to do whatever the Lord would allow, and practiced extreme self-denial, to save lost souls (9:19-27).

They needed to learn, from the Old Testament examples, the danger of involvement in idolatry (10:1-13). These Christians had no business going to the idol temples or knowingly eating meat offered to idols (10:14-33).

QUESTIONS

8. What is the only lawful means of fulfilling sexual desire (7:1-5; Hebrews 13:4)?______________________________

   ____

9. What two options are available to individuals who divorce (7:11)?_______

   ____

   ____

10. What can our liberties become if we misuse them (8:9-12)? ___________

    ____

    ____

11. Despite his rights, what had Paul made himself to be, and why (9:19)?

    ____

    ____

    ____

12. What warning is given in 1 Corinthians 10:12?____________________

    ____

    ____

    ____

13. What promise is given in verse 13? __________________________

    ____

    ____

14. What admonition is given in verse 31? ______________________________
____
____
____

The Head Covering and the Lord's Supper (Chapter 11)

The worship was being disrupted by women who failed to keep the Corinthian custom of wearing a head covering during the assembly (11:2-11). It is apparent that Paul is addressing a local custom, not a universal God-given command (11:16).

The Lord's Supper is a solemn memorial of the Lord's suffering and death on the cross for our sins. The church was turning this memorial into an observance that resembled the drunken feasts they previously enjoyed at their idol's temples. Paul stopped this sinful practice and set forth the proper way the church was to observe this memorial (11:17-34).

The Miraculous Gifts of the Holy Spirit (Chapters 12-14)

Some church members had received gifts from the Holy Spirit. Unfortunately, they were using these gifts as a means of promoting themselves and further dividing the church.

Paul described some of the different gifts and explained that they were all given by the same Holy Spirit (12:4-11). The church members needed to work together as a functioning body, not against one another as rivals or enemies (12:12-31).

While they admired these miraculous gifts (especially the gift of tongues), Paul explained that love is the greatest gift a Christian can possess and exercise (13:1-13). He went on to explain how to use all miraculous gifts, including the gift of tongues (14:1-40). Although we no longer have these gifts, these instructions are important because they tell us how to conduct our worship assemblies.

QUESTIONS

15. In the context of chapter 11, explain what it means to partake of the Lord's Supper in an unworthy manner (11:27). ______________________
____
____
____

16. How had these Christians received their spiritual gifts (Acts 8:18-19; Romans 1:11)? ______________________

17. To what is the local church compared (12:12-31)? ______________________

18. In your own words, explain why love is the greatest gift. ______________________

19. What rule must govern our worship assemblies (14:40)? ______________________

The Resurrection (Chapters 15)

Some members were denying that there would be a personal, bodily resurrection from the grave. Paul showed how Christ's resurrection was a part of the gospel, which they had already received (15:1-4). Jesus' bodily resurrection was verified by numerous eyewitnesses (15:5-11), being the foundation of our faith (15:12-19), and proving our own future bodily resurrection (15:20-34). Paul went on to explain, as best he could, what the resurrection would be like (15:35-58).

The Collection and Farewell (Chapter 16)

During this journey, Paul was making a collection for the poor saints in Jerusalem. In his commands about their participation in this effort, he gave the most detailed instructions we have regarding how a local church is to collect the funds it needs to continue its work (16:1-2).

Paul closed the letter with his travel plans (vv. 5-12), final exhortations (vv. 13-18), and greetings to and from brethren (vv. 19-24).

QUESTIONS

20. What warning is given in 1 Corinthians 15:33? ______________________

21. What will happen to those who are still alive when the Lord returns (15:50-53)? ______________________________
____
____

22. What were the church members to do when they assembled on the first day of the week (16:2)?______________________________
____
____
____

The church in Corinth had incredible problems, but it was still recognized as a faithful local church (1:2). This tells us there are no church problems so big that they can't be addressed and solved. However, it requires all members to respect Christ's authority, honor His word above their own personal rights, repent of their sins, and be of the same mind and the same judgment.

Lesson 3

Second Corinthians

Highlights

We walk by faith, not by sight (2 Corinthians 5:7).

We must all appear before the judgement seat of Christ (2 Corinthians 5:10).

Do not be unequally yoked together with unbelievers (2 Corinthians. 6:14).

Godly sorrow produces repentance leading to salvation (2 Corinthians 7:10).

Instructions regarding giving (2 Corinthians 8-9).

Examine yourselves (2 Corinthians 13:5).

Author

Paul authored this epistle.

Date

56-57 AD

Paul wrote Second Corinthians within a year after he wrote First Corinthians. Still on his third missionary journey, he had traveled from Ephesus into Macedonia. Most likely, he wrote this epistle from Philippi (Acts 20:1) and sent it ahead to Corinth.

Purpose

To defend the work Paul had done in Corinth.

Second Corinthians is Paul's most personal and emotional letter. It provides insight into Paul's mind as he deals with sorrow, uncertainty, disappointment and personal attacks on his character.

His first letter to Corinth was very harsh. While he was still in Ephesus, Paul sent Titus to Corinth

Spotlight

Paul's defense.

Now then, we are **ambassadors** for Christ, as though God were **pleading** through us: we **implore** you on Christ's behalf, be **reconciled** to God.

- 2 Corinthians 5:20

to bring back word of how they had received the letter. He was so concerned that he didn't wait for Titus to return. He started traveling toward Corinth (2:12-13). He finally met Titus in Macedonia (7:5-7). The news about the church in Corinth was mixed. Most of the members had repented and begun dealing with the problems. However, two new problems were brought to Paul's attention.

First, the church was not preparing its collection for the poor saints in Jerusalem (1 Corinthians 16:1-2). They needed to complete this collection before Paul arrived (chapters 8-9); otherwise, both Paul and the church members would be put to shame before those who were traveling with him.

Second, Judaizing teachers had come to Corinth and attempted to poison the church members' minds against Paul. A Judaizing teacher was a Jewish Christian who insisted that, to be a true disciple, Gentile Christians must be circumcised and keep the Law of Moses (Acts 15:5).

The truth regarding this matter had been settled by the apostles and elders of the church in Jerusalem. Gentiles did not have to be circumcised and keep the Law of Moses to be saved (Acts 15). Unfortunately, this did not stop the Judaizers from their efforts. Because Paul worked primarily among Gentiles and was so successful, Judaizers followed him and tried to undermine his work.

Second Corinthians tells us they challenged Paul's authority and apostleship by attacking his character and questioning his motives. They said he was not a man of his word (1:17-19). They accused him of writing strong letters but being weak in appearance and not able or willing to back up his threats (10:10). They even said he was either insulting them by not accepting financial support (11:7) or was setting them up so he could take from them a great sum of money in the form of the collection for the saints (12:16-18).

Throughout the epistle, Paul defended himself against these charges, not for his own sake, but

Clearly you are an **epistle** of Christ, **ministered** by us, written not with **ink** but by the **Spirit** of the living God, not on tablets of **stone** but on tablets of **flesh**, that is, of the **heart**.

- 2 Corinthians 3:3

for the sake of his work as an apostle and the faithfulness of the church in Corinth. He expressed disappointment over having to do this. The Corinthians themselves should have defended Paul and driven out the false teachers (3:1-3; 12:11-12).

Second Corinthians is not easy to read. It is not as organized as First Corinthians. Paul's topics overlap as he deals with the primary issues of defending his ministry (chapters 1-7), preparing the collection (chapters 8-9), and defending his apostleship (chapters 10-13).

Paul Defends His Ministry (Chapters 1-7)

Paul was greatly comforted when he learned how the Corinthians had received his first letter (1:3-14). He answered the charge that he was not a man of his word, stating that he had intended to come to them, but it turned out to be best that he not do so at that time (1:15-24).

In First Corinthians, Paul commanded them to put away a brother who was in sin (1 Corinthians 5). The majority of the members had responded by obeying and addressing this matter (2 Corinthians 2:6-11). The brother had repented, which was the desired response. Paul instructed them to forgive, comfort and reaffirm their love for him. He was to be restored to their fellowship.

The Judaizers took great pride in the Law of Moses. In chapter 3, Paul identified himself as a minister of the new covenant (3:6) and showed how this new covenant (the gospel of Christ) is superior to the old covenant (the Law of Moses).

THE OLD	THE NEW
Written on stone	Written on the heart (v. 3)
Ministry of death and condemnation	Ministry of the Spirit and righteousness (vv. 7-9)
Done away	Remains (v. 11)

QUESTIONS

1. What was a Judaizer? What did they teach? ______________________________

____

____

____

2. What did the Judaizers do to Paul? ______________________________

____

____

3. How does Paul describe God in 2 Corinthians 1:3? ____________________

____

____

4. What three things must they do for the man who had repented (2:7-8)?

____

____

____

5. State three things that make the New Covenant superior to the Old (3:3, 7-9, 11). __________________________________

____

____

Paul and the other apostles suffered greatly because of their ministry. They were not figureheads looking to receive praise and adoration from men. They were mere earthen vessels that held the gospel treasure for all mankind (4:7). They were willing to endure hardships for the sake of those who would be saved because of their efforts (4:15).

Paul walked by faith, not by sight (5:7). He did not dwell on the abundance of his sufferings; rather, he focused his attention on eternal blessings. This allowed him to view his sufferings as light, momentary afflictions (4:17-18). Paul anticipated a better existence in his life to come (5:1-6).

To Paul, pleasing God was the most important thing. Because of this, he was faithful to his ministry—calling men to be reconciled to God (5:9-21). When men respond by obeying the gospel, they become new creatures who are prepared to stand before the judgment seat of Christ.

A Christian has no business enjoying the sins of the world, nor should he associate with a non-Christian in any way that would compromise his fellowship with God and his influence upon the world. Paul pleaded with the Corinthians not to receive God's grace in vain. It was time for them to abandon the world around them and separate themselves from sin (6:1-7:1).

Paul wrote the first letter to get them to repent. Having received a full report from Titus, Paul was thankful that his efforts were largely successful (7:2-12). Confronting a person in sin is not pleasant. It can cause great sorrow. However, if it is godly sorrow, it will bring repentance and lead to salvation. Worldly sorrow leads only to death. This passage helps us understand that repentance is not just feeling bad about our sins, but turning from them and reforming our conduct.

QUESTIONS

6. Who blinds the minds of men so they will not believe the gospel and be saved (4:3-4)? ____________________

7. Paul said, "we have this treasure in earthen vessels" (4:7). What is the treasure and what are the earthen vessels? ____________________

8. How did Paul describe the things he had suffered during his ministry (4:17)?

9. How was Paul able to look beyond his physical sufferings and see the glory that awaited him (5:7)? ____________________

10. Why must everyone be reconciled to God (5:10)? ____________________

11. What is produced by godly sorrow (7:10)? ____________________

The Collection (Chapters 8-9)

In chapters 8-9, Paul breaks from defending himself and his ministry to address their lack of preparation concerning the collection for the poor saints in Jerusalem.

They needed to prepare this collection. Paul was coming to them with messengers from other churches that had already contributed to this effort. The Corinthians' commitment to participate in this benevolence had encouraged many of these other churches to get involved and to give generously above their means. If Paul and these messengers arrived in Corinth and found them unprepared, the Corinthians would be ashamed!

Paul instructed them to give bountifully, purposely, cheerfully, and liberally (2 Corinthians 9:6-7, 11). In turn, they could trust God to supply all their needs.

QUESTIONS

12. What motivated the poor Macedonians to give beyond their means (8:5)?

____

____

13. What does it mean to "give as he purposes in his heart" (9:7)? _________

____

____

14. What did Jesus say about giving (Acts 20:35)? ______________________

____

____

Paul Defends His Apostleship (Chapters 10-13)

One of the criticisms made against Paul was that he was weak in appearance (10:10). Paul let them know his physical size and speaking ability did not matter. He was fighting a spiritual battle, and the weapons of his warfare were mighty for destroying everything that exalted itself against Christ (10:3-6).

Using sarcasm, Paul complimented the Corinthians for tolerating the teaching of a false gospel (11:4), accepting the boasting of the Judaizers (11:16-19), and allowing themselves to be swindled and brought into bondage (11:20-21).

Paul detailed many of his sufferings for the cause of Christ (11:22-33). This list is a source of encouragement for us as we endure hardships for Christ. Because this epistle was written in the middle of Paul's ministry, it contains only a partial list of the things he suffered for the cause of Christ. Everything Paul suffered after Acts 20:2 occurred after he wrote this epistle.

Paul added to his credentials by speaking of a great revelation he was privileged to receive from God. He was so uncomfortable boasting about this experience that he spoke of himself in the third person (12:1-6).

Because this great experience could cause him to exalt himself, the Lord gave Paul a thorn in the flesh to make him humble (12:7-10). Three times Paul pleaded with the Lord to remove this thorn. Instead, he was made to understand that he needed the infirmity and would be given the strength to endure it. We don't know what Paul's thorn in the flesh was, but this actually works to our advantage. We can apply Paul's experience to our own sufferings. God does not always take away the thorns in our flesh, but He gives us the strength to endure them.

Paul closed his letter with a warning. They needed to test themselves to be sure they were prepared for his visit (13:1-10). Those who prepared themselves would stand complete, while those who didn't would see full proof of his apostolic power and authority.

QUESTIONS

15. Describe what the weapons of our spiritual warfare are able to do (10:4-5). ____________________

16. Who stands approved before God (10:18)? ____________________

17. Describe the suffering Paul experienced for the cause of Christ (11:23-28). ____________________

18. Why didn't the Lord remove Paul's thorn in the flesh (12:7-10)? ____________________

19. What must all Christians do (13:5)? Why? ____________________

Second Corinthians is an important part of the New Testament. In addition to addressing several important topics, it allows us to gain insight into Paul's heart as he defends his ministry, his character, and the Corinthians.

Lesson 4

Galatians

Highlights

"But even if we, or an angel from heaven, preach any other gospel to you than what we have preached to you, let him be accursed" (1:8).

"I have been crucified with Christ; it is no longer I who live, but Christ lives in me..." (2:20).

"For as many of you as were baptized into Christ have put on Christ" (3:27).

The works of the flesh (5:19-21).

The fruit of the Spirit (5:22-23).

Author

Paul authored this epistle.

Date

The exact date of this epistle is uncertain.

Because the contents of the letter are similar to Second Corinthians and Romans, some believe they could have been written around the same time: 57-58 AD.

Purpose

To encourage Gentile Christians not to follow the Law of Moses.

This letter was not written to a local church (such as the church in Rome or Corinth). It was written to a number of local churches in Asia Minor's northeastern region called Galatia. Acts records Paul's passage through this area on his second and

Spotlight

Do not be entangled again with a yoke of bondage.

Stand fast therefore in the **liberty** by which Christ has made us **free**, and do not be **entangled** again with a yoke of **bondage**.

- Galatians 5:1

third journeys (Acts 16:6; 18:23) but does not give any details of his work there.

These people welcomed Paul, and they readily accepted the gospel. After he left them, Judaizers came into their midst and sought to turn them away from the truth. Paul was concerned that his work among them would be for nothing. These Judaizers were preaching an entirely different gospel which, if believed and followed, would cost the Galatians their eternal salvation. This was an emergency situation. The book of Galatians does not contain Paul's usual greetings. Instead, it gets right to the point, addresses the problems, and admonishes these Christians to do the right thing.

This book can be divided into three sections: Paul defends his apostleship (chapters 1-2), Paul defends their freedom in Christ (3:1-5:6), and Paul admonishes them regarding proper use of that freedom (5:7-6:18).

Beloved, do not **believe** every spirit, but **test** the spirits, whether they are of **God**; because many **false prophets** have gone out into the **world**.

- 1 John 4:1

Paul Defends His Apostleship (Chapters 1-2)

After a brief introduction (1:1-5), Paul expressed his amazement that they had turned away from the truth to accept a perverted gospel (1:6-10). Instead of testing and rejecting the Judaizers' false doctrine (1 Thessalonians 5:21-22; 1 John 4:1; Revelation 2:2), the Galatians accepted their teachings.

While open-mindedness is a virtue in today's world, God expects us to stand firm in His truth. We must reject all teaching that is contrary to the gospel, regardless of its source.

The Judaizers suggested that Paul had made himself an apostle and had learned his message from men. He addressed these false charges by giving a detailed summary of his call and training as an apostle.

Paul had been a great enemy to the cause of Christ (1:13-15). After his conversion in Damascus, he did not go to Jerusalem to study with the apostles. He went to Arabia where, like the original 12 apostles, he was personally taught by the Lord (1:11-12, 16-17). After three years, he made a trip to Jerusalem, but spent little time with Peter, and was virtually unknown by the churches in that area (1:18-24).

After 14 years, he returned to Jerusalem with Barnabas and Titus. He did not go to receive instruction from the apostles, but to confer with them concerning preaching the gospel to the Gentiles (2:1-10). The apostles acknowledged that this work, which Paul was doing without their training or their commission, was the Lord's work.

As further evidence of his apostolic authority, Paul spoke of a time when he publicly rebuked Peter (2:11-21). Only another apostle could have done this with God's approval.

QUESTIONS

1. Who were the Judaizers and what did they teach (Acts 15:1, 5)? You may want to refer to lesson 3 to review this subject. ____________________

   ____

   ____

   ____

2. What amazed Paul (Galatians 1:6)? ____________________

   ____

   ____

3. Who made Paul an apostle (1:1)? ____________________

   ____

   ____

4. From whom did Paul receive the gospel he preached (1:11-12)? __________

   ____

5. Explain why Paul withstood Peter to his face in Antioch (2:11-14). ________

   ____

   ____

   ____

6. How does Paul describe the extent of his commitment to Christ (2:20)?

   ____

   ____

   ____

Paul Defends Their Freedom in Christ (3:1-5:6)

Someone had bewitched or fooled these Galatians (2:1). There was no logical explanation for their rejecting the gospel in favor of the Law of Moses. Paul asked them to think back to how they were saved. Were they saved by the works of the Law of Moses or through faith in Jesus Christ? Through Christ, they had been set free from their sins but were now in danger of placing themselves under bondage to the Law of Moses.

The Jews looked up to Abraham. He was the father of their nation. Abraham was justified by his faith before God gave the Law of Moses. Not only that, but God used Abraham's faith as the means of saving the Gentiles (3:6-9). This promise is recorded in Genesis 12:1-3.

The Law of Moses cannot save. This law placed men under a curse because it identified sin and condemned those who were in violation (3:10-14). Christ's sacrifice, not the Law of Moses, made salvation possible.

The Law of Moses did not nullify or replace God's promise to Abraham (3:15-18). The Law was not for the purpose of saving mankind, but to prepare mankind to accept Christ—the fulfillment of God's promise to Abraham (3:19-29). It served as a tutor, or schoolmaster, to bring the Jews to Christ where they could be justified by faith just as their father Abraham. Both Jews and Gentiles were made one in Christ through faith and baptism. God's promise to Abraham to save all people through faith was still in effect while the Law of Moses was serving its temporary purpose.

The Law of Moses served its purpose. Christ came to redeem those who were under the law. They are no longer slaves but adopted sons who share in the inheritance found in Christ (4:1-7).

Paul used various arguments to show that all who are free in Christ must not be brought under bondage to the Law of Moses (4:8-31). Circumcision, as a religious act, would obligate the Galatians to keep all of the Law. Such would separate them from the salvation they had obtained in Christ and cause them to fall from grace (5:1-6).

QUESTIONS

7. What promise did God make to Abraham in Genesis 12:3? ____________

____

____

8. Who did God plan to justify by faith (Galatians 3:8)? ____________

____

9. Why isn't salvation found in the Law of Moses? Explain this Law's purpose (3:10, 19, 23-25).____
____
____
____

10. Did the Law of Moses invalidate or set aside God's promise to Abraham (3:17)? ____

11. What action places us in Christ (3:27)?____
____
____

12. Explain the danger these Galatians would encounter if they proceeded with keeping the Law of Moses (5:1-4).____
____
____

Paul Admonishes Them Regarding Proper Use of Their Freedom (5:7-6:18)

Paul warned the Galatians that they must use the freedom they had in Christ in a worthy manner. Instead of turning against one another, and biting and devouring one another, they needed to love one another. They were not set free to serve themselves and fulfill their own fleshly desires. They were to use their freedom as an opportunity to serve one another in love (5:7-15).

The flesh and the spirit are opposed to each other. Paul identified many of the works of the flesh and said those who practice such things will not inherit the kingdom of God (5:16-21). In contrast, there is no law against bearing the fruit of the spirit: love, joy, peace, longsuffering, kindness, goodness, faithfulness, gentleness, and self-control (5:22-26).

Standing fast in their liberty required these Galatians to be mindful of one another. They were to restore those who were overtaken in sins and help those who were laboring under heavy burdens, while carrying their own weight so as not to burden others (6:1-5). They were to share with those who taught them and with those who were in need, and not grow weary while doing good, knowing they would reap what they sowed (6:6-10).

Paul closed the letter with a final appeal for them to reject the Judaizers' efforts and to accept him as a genuine apostle (6:11-18).

QUESTIONS

13. How were the Galatians to use their liberty in Christ (5:13-15)?________

____

____

14. What two "masters" battle for control of our hearts (5:16-17)? ________

____

____

15. What are the consequences of habitually practicing the works of the flesh (5:19-21)? ______________________________

____

16. List the fruit of the Spirit (5:22-23).______________________________

____

____

____

17. What are we to do for a brother who is overtaken in a sin (6:1)?________

____

____

18. What are we to do for a brother who is struggling with a burden (6:2)?

____

____

____

19. What lesson is taught in Galatians 6:7-8? ______________________

____

____

____

Galatians is an urgent letter. These Christians were about to cut themselves off from Christ and enter the hopeless bondage of the Law of Moses. While we may not struggle with returning to the Law of Moses, we need to understand that accepting any error contrary to the pure gospel of Jesus Christ will bring us under bondage and cause us to fall from God's grace.

Lesson 5

Ephesians

Highlights

All spiritual blessings are found in Christ (1:3-14).

Christ is head over the church, which is His body (1:22-23).

Salvation by grace through faith (2:8-9).

God's manifold wisdom is made known through the church (3:10).

The unity of the Spirit (4:3-6).

Responsibilities of husbands, wives and children (5:22-6:4).

The whole armor of God (6:10-17).

Author

Paul authored this epistle.

Date

62-63 AD

Ephesians is one of Paul's "prison epistles" written while he was a prisoner in Rome (Acts 28). During this imprisonment, he also wrote Philippians, Colossians and Philemon.

Purpose

To set forth the greatness of the Lord's church and every member's responsibility to walk worthy of this greatness.

This letter does not address any specific problems with the church in Ephesus; rather, it discusses

Spotlight

Through Christ, God has saved both Jews and Gentiles in one body (the church).

Now to Him who is **able** to do exceedingly abundantly **above** all that we **ask** or **think**, according to the **power** that works in us, to Him be **glory** in the **church** by Christ Jesus to all **generations**, forever and ever. Amen.

- Ephesians 3:20-21

the church's purpose and manner of edification. Because it lacks personal greetings, which are common in many of Paul's letters, some believe that it was meant to be a "general" epistle to be circulated throughout Asia Minor, beginning at Ephesus.

Sin separates man from God. The Law of Moses separated Jews (God's people) from Gentiles. Now, in Christ, God has united both Jews and Gentiles into one body as His saved people—the church. Paul spends the first half of this epistle explaining in detail how God brought about this great work of redemption. The second half of the epistle contains practical instructions regarding how Christians are to conduct themselves, both in the local church and in their personal lives.

Blessed be the **God** and **Father** of our Lord Jesus Christ, who has **blessed** us with every **spiritual** blessing in the **heavenly** places in **Christ**.

- Ephesians 1:3

Spiritual Blessings in Christ (1:3-14)

Paul began this epistle by listing "every spiritual blessing" available in Christ. God chose Christ to be the means through which He offered these blessings to mankind.

1. God chose us (v. 4). He has chosen to claim those who are in His Son.
2. We are adopted as sons (v. 5). It was God's plan to willingly make us, through Christ, a part of His spiritual family.
3. We become acceptable to God (v. 6). Left to ourselves, because of our sin, we would be completely unacceptable.
4. We have redemption, the forgiveness of sins (v. 7). To redeem means to buy back. We were lost to God because we sinned. Christ's blood is the price paid to buy us back. This blood is the sacrifice offered for forgiveness of our sins.
5. We have the mystery of God's will revealed to us (v. 9). Before the foundation of the world, God planned to save all men through Christ, but

His plan remained a mystery to man until it was revealed through the preaching of the gospel.

6. We have obtained an inheritance (v. 11). Now that we are in God's family, we share in an inheritance—eternal life in heaven.
7. We are sealed with the Holy Spirit (v. 13). A seal is a mark of ownership. All who are in Christ receive the Holy Spirit. In the spiritual realm, we are marked, or identified, as belonging to God.

When, through baptism, one enters a relationship with Christ (Galatians 3:27), he receives every spiritual blessing God offers through Christ.

Christ is Head of the Church (1:15-23)

Paul mentioned his prayer for them. He wanted them to grow in their knowledge and understanding of their great blessings in Christ. God's power to help them is exceedingly great and mighty. He demonstrated this same power when He raised Christ from the dead, seated Him at His right hand, put all things under His authority and made Him head over all things that pertain to the church. The church is the body of Christ, and this body has only one head—Christ.

QUESTIONS

1. Where, or in whom, are all spiritual blessings found (1:3)? ____________

   ____

2. How does one get into Christ (Galatians 3:27)? ____________

   ____

3. Who is head of the Church (1:22-23)? ____________

Jew and Gentile Are Reconciled to God in One Body (Chapter 2)

Paul described their pitiful, sinful condition (vs. 1-3). They were dead, walking after their lusts, and deserving of God's wrath. God, motivated by His mercy, love and grace, acted to save them (vs. 4-10). Salvation cannot be earned by merit. It is a gift to be received through faith.

The church in Ephesus was likely made up mostly of Gentiles. Having been separated from God's covenant people (the Jews), the Gentiles were in a hopeless condition before God. They were aliens from the commonwealth of Israel, strangers from the covenants of promise, having no hope and without God in the world (vv. 11-12).

The Gentiles are now brought near to God by the blood of Christ (vv. 13-18). For centuries, the Law of Moses was a wall that separated the two groups. Jesus' death on the cross fulfilled God's purpose for this Law and took it out of the way, thus breaking down the wall of separation. These two groups of people, now united into one, are reconciled to God in one body. Our study of other epistles has shown that some Jewish Christians had a difficult time overcoming this change. We do not struggle with this issue today, but we do need to realize and appreciate the fact that the gospel of Christ breaks down some barriers that otherwise separate people.

Paul pictured the church as a spiritual temple in which the individual members were stones placed together upon the foundation of Christ, His apostles, and His prophets (vv. 19-22). This would have been a relevant illustration to the Christians in Ephesus. That city was home to the temple of Diana, one of the seven wonders of the ancient world. It was 450 feet long, 225 feet wide, and 60 feet high, with more than 127 columns. This temple enjoyed the loyal devotion of the citizens of Ephesus (Acts 19:23-41). It could have been discouraging for these Christians to continue their spiritual service to God in the shadow of such an impressive structure admired by everyone around them. Paul let them know they were part of the holy temple of the true and living God.

QUESTIONS

4. What three things moved God to save us from our sins (2:4-5)?________

   ____

   ____

5. Can we ever earn our salvation? How, and upon what grounds, does God offer salvation (2:8-9)?________________________

   ____

   ____

   ____

6. Describe the hopeless condition of the Gentiles while the Law of Moses was in effect (2:11-13). ________________________

   ____

   ____

7. What did Christ's death enable God to do with Jews and Gentiles (2:14-16)?

   ____

   ____

8. How did Paul describe the local church (2:19-22)?____________

9. Explain why this description would have been important to the Ephesians. ____________

The Mystery of the Gospel (Chapter 3)

The joining of Jews and Gentiles into one saved body is the great mystery of the Gospel. These two groups had been separated for centuries. However, it was not God's eternal purpose to separate mankind, but to save all in one body in Christ (the church). "That the Gentiles should be fellow heirs, of the same body, and partakers of His promise in Christ through the gospel" (v. 6). In doing so, the church displays God's manifold wisdom (v. 10-11). He is to be glorified in the church by Christ Jesus to all generations (v. 21).

QUESTIONS

10. What did Paul promise the readers of this epistle (3:4)? ____________

11. What eternal plan came about through the gospel (3:6)?____________

Working in Unity with Other Christians (4:1-16)

Paul set forth the grounds for unity within the local church. There are seven "ones" upon which there must be agreement: one *body, Spirit, hope, Lord, faith, baptism* and *God* (vv. 3-6). Members of the local church must work together with the right attitudes to accomplish God's work. Every member is to contribute his or her unique gifts and talents to the growth and edification of the church.

QUESTIONS

12. What attitudes are Christians to show toward one another (4:2)? ____________

13. Identify the seven "ones" upon which the unity of the Spirit must be founded and maintained (4:4-6).___________________________________

14. What results from the unity and joint efforts of every church member (4:16)? ___________________________________

The Christian's Walk (4:17-5:21)

The word *walk* has to do with the way one lives his daily life. Members of the Lord's church cannot live however they want. Paul instructs us to put off the old man of sin and put on a new man who has been renewed regarding how he thinks and acts (4:17-32).

We are to walk in love, as Christ loved us and gave Himself for us (vs. 1-2). We are not to join in the world's sins. We are to walk in light, doing things that are acceptable to God (vs. 3-14). Finally, we are to walk in wisdom, understanding the will of the Lord (vs. 15-21).

QUESTIONS

15. What were the Ephesians to put off and to put on (4:22-24)? __________

16. List some of the things Christians can no longer do (4:25-29).__________

17. What did Paul say about people who are fornicators, unclean, or covetous (5:5)? ___________________________________

Personal Relationships (5:22-6:9)

Christianity impacts every facet of our lives. Paul gave instructions regarding the husband and wife relationship (5:22-33) and the relationship between parents and children (6:1-4). Paul even gave instructions to Christians who were slaves and to those who were masters (vv. 5-9).

QUESTIONS

18. What is the wife's responsibility toward her husband (5:22, 24, 33)?

19. What is the husband's responsibility toward his wife (5: 25, 28, 33)?

20. What responsibility did God give to children (6:1)?

21. In your own words, explain how children honor their parents.

22. What responsibility do fathers (parents) have toward their children (6:4)?

Arming Ourselves for Spiritual Battle (6:10-20)

Christians are to be strong in the Lord and put on the whole armor of God. Paul wrote this epistle while a prisoner at Rome. He likely would have seen Roman soldiers every day. The armor of God was modeled after that of a Roman soldier. This armor enables us to fight, resist and withstand Satan's efforts to destroy us.

QUESTIONS

23. Identify the six pieces of the armor of God (6:14-17).

24. Why must we wear this armor (vv. 11-13)?

Conclusion

The book of Ephesians is an important part of the New Testament. It sets forth the work that God did, from the foundation of the world, to save us from our sins and join all people together in the church. Then it sets forth our responsibilities as God's saved people, living, working and worshipping together as His church.

Lesson 6

Philippians

Highlights

"To live is Christ, and to die is gain" (1:21).

Jesus is the humbled, and exalted, Christ (2:5-11).

Pressing toward the upward call of Christ (3:7-14).

Our citizenship is in Heaven (3:20).

Prayer and the peace of God (4:6-7).

Think on these things (4:8).

"I can do all things through Christ who strengthens me" (4:13).

Author

Paul authored this epistle.

Date

62-63 AD

This is one of Paul's "prison epistles" written while he was a prisoner in Rome (Acts 28). During this imprisonment, he also wrote Ephesians, Colossians and Philemon.

Purpose

Paul expressed his joy and gratitude to the Philippians. This church had a special relationship with Paul in that they faithfully sent him financial support as he preached the gospel (Philippians 4:15-16).

Paul established the church in Philippi during his second missionary journey (Acts 16:11-40). Philippi was a Roman colony. It was maintained primarily

Spotlight

Rejoice!

Rejoice in the Lord **always**. Again I will say, **rejoice**!

- Philippians 4:4

as a military post and a means of spreading the Roman way of life further to the east. Although they were located in Macedonia, the citizens of Philippi took great pride in living and acting as Romans.

The epistle does not contain any serious rebukes or indicate any serious problems in the church at Philippi. The members appear to be at peace, both without and within. Instead, Philippians contains a series of reasons for these Christians to rejoice. Forms of the words "joy" and "rejoice" are found 15 times in this letter. What made these admonitions even more significant was the fact they came from one who seemingly had no reason to rejoice. Paul was an innocent prisoner awaiting an uncertain future, but his faith in God allowed him to find reasons to rejoice in his immediate circumstances. Because of Paul's attitude, many people say Philippians is their favorite book of the Bible.

The Fruits of Paul's Imprisonment (Chapter 1)

Paul began the epistle by speaking of his great love for this congregation. They had helped in his efforts to preach the gospel in various places. He prayed for their love to abound in knowledge and discernment, and that they would be fruitful and without offense to God's glory (vv. 3-11).

Paul had a great desire to go to Rome (Romans 1:8-13; 15:23-24). He finally made it, but not in a way he could have imagined. He was a prisoner awaiting a hearing before Caesar.

Despite these circumstances, Paul assured the Philippians that God had used his imprisonment as a means of furthering the gospel (vv. 12-18).

- Being a prisoner gave Paul an audience with many who otherwise would not have heard him (v. 13).
- His boldness as a prisoner encouraged others to be bold in their preaching (v. 14).

For to me, to **live** is **Christ**, and to **die** is **gain**.

- Philippians 1:21

- Those who sought to do him harm were talking about the gospel, and thus helping to further spread its saving message and bring glory to God (vv. 15-16).

We need to learn from Paul's attitude toward this situation. Things do not always go the way we want, but we must learn to see how God is able to use even the most adverse circumstances in our lives to further His gospel and save lost souls.

The outcome of Paul's hearing before Caesar was uncertain, but Paul was not troubled over this situation. If released, he knew he would continue to help Christians. If executed, he would go to be with the Lord. Either way, God would be glorified (vv. 19-26).

Regardless of what happened to Paul, the important thing was that the Christians in Philippi continue to conduct themselves in a manner worthy of the gospel. They were to stand united in their efforts to bravely advance the gospel of Christ (vv. 27-30).

QUESTIONS

1. How had the church in Philippi helped Paul in his efforts to spread the gospel (1:5; 2:25-30; 4:15-16)? ______________________________

____

____

____

2. What was Paul's prayer for the Philippians (1:9-11)? ______________

____

____

3. Explain how it was to the gospel's advantage that Paul had come to Rome as a prisoner and not as a free man (vv. 12-18). ____________

____

____

____

4. Name some times when your life has not gone as expected, yet things turned out for the better. ______________________________

____

____

____

____

5. Explain how death would be gain for Paul (vv. 21-23).

6. Regardless of the outcome of Paul's trial, what did he expect of the Philippians (v. 27)?

Exhortations to the Philippians (2:1-18)

Paul admonished these Christians to maintain their unity by humbly putting the needs of others before their own (vv. 1-4).

Jesus is the perfect example of this necessary mindset. He put our needs before His own. Although He is God, Jesus came into this world as a bondservant and humbled Himself to the point of death to secure our salvation. Because of this humble obedience, God has exalted Him. Every knee should, and will, bow, and every tongue should, and will, confess that Jesus Christ is Lord (vv. 5-11; Romans 14:11).

Paul admonished the Philippians to work out their own salvation with fear and trembling (vv. 12-18). With or without Paul in their future, they were to see their Christian walk through to the end and live as lights in a crooked and perverse world of darkness.

QUESTIONS

7. Describe the characteristics that are necessary to maintain unity in a local congregation (2:2-4).

8. How did Jesus demonstrate His willingness to put the needs of others before His own (vv. 5-8)?

9. What has God done for Jesus because of His willingness to humble Himself and obey (vv. 9-11)?

10. What does it mean to "work out your own salvation" (v. 12)? Did Paul expect them to earn their salvation or to see it through to the end?

11. What were the responsibilities of these Christians who were in "the midst of a crooked and perverse generation" (v. 15)?

Timothy and Epaphroditus (2:19-30)

Timothy was one of Paul's trusted companions. He was with Paul when he established the church in Philippi (Acts 16:1-3, 12). He had faithfully served the Lord with Paul as a son would with his father. Paul would send Timothy to them as soon as he learned the outcome of his hearing before Caesar, and Timothy would be an added encouragement to them.

Epaphroditus was from Philippi. He had brought a gift from them to Paul in Rome (4:18). He became sick and nearly died while he was there. God showed His mercy in that He allowed Epaphroditus to recover. Now that he was better, he wanted to return to Philippi so the brethren there could be relieved to see him again. Paul sent this letter to the church in Philippi with Epaphroditus.

QUESTIONS

12. Why do you think Paul felt confident in sending Timothy to Philippi (vv. 20-22)?

13. Why did Paul feel compelled to send Epaphroditus back to Philippi (vv. 25-28)?

Warnings Against False Teachers (Chapter 3)

As we have noted in previous lessons, Paul had to warn various churches about Judaizing teachers who sought to turn Gentile Christians away from the truth of the gospel by compelling them to be circumcised and to keep the Law of Moses. He identified these Judaizers as "dogs," "evil workers" and "the mutilation" (v. 2).

Paul had willingly forsaken everything about which these Judaizers found reasons to boast (vv. 3-6). He counted these fleshly heritages and achievements as loss for the knowledge of Christ. To Paul, nothing was more important than gaining Christ, having the righteousness that is through faith in Christ, living for Christ and attaining the resurrection from the dead (vv. 7-11).

Paul did not see himself as having attained this goal. He was not satisfied with his level of spiritual maturity. He forgot the things that were left behind him and pressed on toward the goal of the upward call of Christ Jesus. This is the goal of every mature Christian, and the Philippians had several examples of men like Paul to follow as the pattern for their spiritual lives (vv. 12-17).

Remember that Philippi was a Roman colony. Those who lived there were Roman citizens, and they conducted themselves as if they were in Rome. Paul reminded these Christians that their citizenship was really in Heaven (vv. 20-4:1). They lived in Philippi, but they needed to conduct themselves as Christians, focusing on their upward calling and the glorious return of their Savior.

QUESTIONS

14. How did Paul view his heritage and his past accomplishments in comparison to the blessings he had found in Christ (3:4-8)? ____________

    ____

    ____

15. Describe Paul's attitude toward obtaining his reward (vv. 12-14).

    ____

    ____

    ____

16. What did Paul mean when he said our citizenship is in heaven (v. 20)?

    ____

    ____

Exhortations (4:2-9)

Paul delivered various exhortations to the Philippians.

- He implored two sisters in Christ to overcome their differences (vv. 2-3).
- The members of the church were to rejoice in the Lord (v. 4).

- They were to conduct themselves in a level-headed manner (v. 5).
- The peace of God was available through prayer, meditating on proper things and following Paul's teaching and example (vv. 6-9).

QUESTIONS

17. In whom are we to rejoice (4:4)?____________________

____

18. What is the peace of God able to do (v. 7)? ________________

____

____

____

19. Explain how meditating on good things can give us peace (v. 9). ________

____

____

____

Their Fellowship with Paul (4:10-20)

Paul closed the epistle by speaking fondly of their efforts to support him in his work. He had learned to be content in various situations he faced as he labored to spread the gospel. Paul knew he could endure any circumstance because of the strength he found in Christ (vv. 10-13).

Despite his ability to go without, he praised the Philippians for continuing to help him as they had from the very beginning. Their latest gift sent to Paul by way of Epaphroditus was a sacrifice acceptable to God, who would continue to richly supply their needs (vv. 14-20).

QUESTIONS

20. What had Paul learned (v. 11)?________________________

____

____

____

21. What confidence did Paul have as he faced adverse circumstances (v. 13)?

____

____

____

22. What great promise did Paul make to the Philippians (v. 19)? ____________

____

____

____

Paul closed this epistle with very encouraging words (vv. 21-23). He sent greetings from all the Christians who were with him in Rome, including those who were "of Caesar's household." Many believe these were servants who attended to Caesar's house. Even though Paul was imprisoned, the gospel was not. It had found its way into the household of the Roman emperor.

Today, the gospel continues to spread across the world and into good and honest hearts. For this, we should "rejoice in the Lord always!"

Lesson 7

Colossians and Philemon

COLOSSIANS

Highlights

The Preeminent Christ (1:15-23).

"In Him dwells the fullness of the Godhead bodily" (2:9).

Love is the bond of perfection (3:14).

"Do all in the name of the Lord Jesus" (4:17).

Author

Paul authored this epistle.

Date

62-63 AD

Colossians is one of Paul's "prison epistles" written while he was a prisoner in Rome (Acts 28). During this imprisonment, he also wrote Philippians, Colossians and Philemon.

Purpose

To confront false doctrines that were threatening the church in Colossae.

Colossae was located 120 miles east of Ephesus. There were two influential cities near Colossae: Laodicea (12 miles to the west) and Hierapolis (13 miles to the northwest). Apparently, there were churches in all three cities (Colossians 4:13, 16).

The book of Acts contains no record of Paul visiting Colossae or establishing the church in that city. The

Spotlight

Complete in Christ.

For in **Him** dwells all the fullness of the **Godhead** bodily; and you are **complete** in Him, who is the **head** of all **principality** and **power**.

- Colossians 2:9-10

For this reason we also, since the day we **heard** it, do not cease to **pray** for you, and to ask that you may be **filled** with the **knowledge** of His will in all **wisdom** and spiritual **understanding**.

- Colossians 1:9

epistle indicates that Paul had only heard of that church (1:4, 7-9), and he noted that many of the members had not personally seen his face (2:1). Likely, the congregation was established by a man named Epaphras (1:7). He was from Colossae (4:12-13). Perhaps he learned the gospel from Paul in Ephesus and took it back to his hometown (Acts 19:10).

Paul had heard of their great faith, but he also learned that several false doctrines were threatening the church. The exact errors troubling the Colossians are not specifically identified, but we can determine their components and sources by looking at Paul's teaching in the epistle.

Ephesians and Colossians

The content of Ephesians and Colossians is similar, especially in the sections that contain practical admonitions (Ephesians 4-6; Colossians 3-4). They can be considered as "sister epistles." However, there is a notable difference which causes each book to stand alone and justifies its inclusion in the New Testament.

Ephesians focuses on the *church* as the functioning body of Christ. The readers were to appreciate God's purpose and design for the church and find their places as working members of a local church.

Colossians places emphasis on *Christ* as head of the church. The readers were to understand that Jesus completely supplied their spiritual needs and to reject every teaching and philosophy that diminished His preeminence.

Paul's Thanksgiving and Prayer for the Colossians (1:1-14)

Paul began this epistle by recalling the prayers and thanksgiving he offered to God because of them. He had heard of their faith in Christ, their love for all Christians, and their hope of heaven. As is the case with all faithful Christians, their reception of the gospel was causing them to bear fruit (vv. 3-8).

However, Paul did not want them to relax their efforts. His constant prayer for their spiritual advancement was quite detailed.

- Be filled with all knowledge of God's will in wisdom and spiritual understanding (v. 9).
- Walk worthy of the Lord, pleasing Him, being fruitful in every good work, increasing in the knowledge of God (v. 10).
- Be strengthened with all might to exercise all patience and longsuffering with joy (v. 11).
- Give thanks to God for allowing them to partake in the inheritance of the saints (v. 12).

God is worthy of our unending gratitude because He has rescued us from Satan (vv. 13-14). He can forgive our sins through the shed blood of Jesus Christ. This allows God to buy us back (redeem us) from the domain of Satan and sin and make us citizens in His Son's kingdom.

The Preeminence of Christ (1:15-23)

Paul's focus now shifts to the main point of his letter—showing how Jesus is superior to all things. Notice the things affirmed about Jesus (vv. 15-20).

- He is the image of the invisible God.
- He is the firstborn over all creation.
- He is the Creator of all things.
- He is before all things.
- He holds all things together.
- He is the head of the church.
- He is the firstborn from the dead.
- He has the preeminence in all things.
- He is the fullness of all things.
- He is the means by which God reconciles all mankind to Himself.

And He is the **head** of the body, the **church**, who is the **beginning**, the **firstborn** from the dead, that in **all** things He may have the **preeminence**.

- Colossians 1:18

The word *reconciliation* means to make friendly again. Sin separates us from God and makes us His enemies. Jesus' blood allows us to have peace with God. After being washed in Jesus' blood, we are holy, blameless, and above reproach in God's sight (vv. 20-22).

This great blessing is conditional (v. 23). We cannot give up on the Lord. We must steadfastly continue in the faith and not allow ourselves to be moved from the hope of the gospel.

Paul's Sufferings and Conflict for the Faith (1:24-29)

Paul spoke of his ministry—carrying the gospel to the Gentiles. God planned to include the Gentiles in His scheme of redemption, but the Jews did not understand this inclusion. Because of this, Paul suffered many things, but his persecution did not deter him from his mission to present every man perfect, complete or mature in Christ Jesus (v. 28).

QUESTIONS

1. How far had the gospel spread by the time Paul wrote this letter (1:5-6)?

   ____

   ____

2. What has Christ delivered us *from* and *into* (v. 13)? ______________

   ____

   ____

3. Paul listed a number of things that prove Christ's superiority over everything (vv. 15-20). Which one do you find most impressive? Why?

   ____

   ____

   ____

   ____

   ____

4. What does the word *reconciliation* mean? ______________

   ____

5. What did Jesus have to do in order to reconcile us to God (vv. 21-22)?

   ____

   ____

   ____

Paul's Defense of the Faith (Chapter 2)

Paul struggled greatly for the spiritual stability and growth of all Christians, including those whom he had never met. His desire was that they be united against all who would deceive them and threaten their standing in Christ (vv. 1-4).

He encouraged them to continue walking in Christ as they had been taught, rooted and built up in Him, established and abounding in the faith (vv. 5-7).

Some who had come into their midst were seeking to take them captive (v. 8). This word is translated from a Greek term that means to be kidnapped or led away as a prisoner. God had already rescued them from bondage (1:13), but they needed to be careful that they were not again made prisoners.

Paul warned of deceitful philosophy, human traditions, and immature speculations. The Colossians did not need any of these things because they were already complete in Christ in Whom dwells all the fullness of the Godhead. They needed nothing more (vv. 9-10). They were to reject those who were coming into their midst and teaching contrary doctrines.

Although not stated specifically, we can gain an understanding of some of these errors that were troubling the Colossians.

JEWISH TRADITIONS (VV. 11-17)

We have noted in previous lessons that Judaizers troubled Paul's work by insisting that the Gentiles be circumcised and keep the Law of Moses. Paul's instructions in these verses addressed errors that came from a Jewish background.

- The Colossians had already undergone the circumcision of Christ during their baptism (vv. 11-13).
- The Law of Moses had been taken out of the way. It was nailed to the Lord's cross (v. 14).
- They were not to let anyone judge them as being unfaithful to God because they failed to observe the ordinances of the Law of Moses (unclean foods, feast days, Sabbaths) (v. 16).
- Moses' Law was a shadow. Christ is the substance of the shadow. His Law is superior (v. 17).

MYSTICAL RELIGIONS (VV. 18-19)

The things mentioned in these two verses were practices associated with the mystical religions of that day: the worship of angels, claims of seeing visions, and daring to speak authoritatively about things not seen. Paul instructed the Colossians to reject these errors and hold fast to Christ.

ASCETICISM (VV. 20-23)

There have always been those who teach that the path to godliness is through extreme self-denial. Denying ourselves of all wholesome pleasures, and purposely inflicting ourselves with pain, are not useful or godly ways to handle fleshly temptations.

QUESTIONS

6. What should bind Christians together (2:2; 3:14)? ____________________

 ____

 ____

7. What does Colossians 2:9 teach concerning Jesus Christ? ____________

 ____

 ____

8. Explain the significance of Christians being made complete in Christ (v. 10). Do we need outside teachings, worldly philosophies, human doctrines, organizations, etc.? ____________________

 ____

 ____

 ____

9. What happened to the Law of Moses (v. 14)? ____________________

 ____

 ____

Guidelines for Christian Living (3:1-4:6)

These Christians were already complete in Christ, and so they must set their minds on things above, where Christ is sitting at God's right hand.

The instructions in this section are very similar to those found in Ephesians 4-6.

- Put off the old man of sin and put on Christ (vv. 5-11)

- Treat members of the church in the proper manner (vv. 12-16).
- Respect Christ's authority (v. 17).
- Maintain obligations to members of your physical family (vv. 18-21).
- Proper behavior of masters and slaves (v. 22-4:1).
- Proper conduct toward those outside the church (vv. 2-6).

QUESTIONS

10. What are we to seek? Where are we to set our minds (3:1-2)? ________

11. What kinds of things will bring God's wrath upon us (vv. 5-6)?________

12. What are we to *put on* (vv. 12-14)?________

13. Explain the obligations family members have toward one another (vv. 18-21).________

Personal Greetings and Instructions (4:7-18)

The epistle ends with a detailed list of names. These verses provide information that helps us better understand some of the people in the New Testament. For instance, we learn that Mark was Barnabas' cousin (v. 10; Acts 12:25; 15:37-39), and that Luke was a doctor (v. 14). This passage also tells us this letter was sent with the letter to Philemon (v. 9).

Paul closed with the instruction to share the epistle with the church in Laodicea (v. 16), indicating that letters written by the apostles were intended to be shared and circulated.

PHILEMON

We are including our study of Philemon with Colossians because these epistles were sent together. Philemon is one of Paul's personal letters. It was not written to a congregation, but to a man named Philemon.

Philemon was a resident of Colossae. We assume he was a wealthy man because the church met in his house (v. 1), he helped Christians (vs. 5-7), and Paul requested that he prepare a place for him to lodge (v. 22). Likely, Paul converted Philemon (v. 19) and considered him a friend and fellow laborer (v. 1, 17).

Philemon owned a slave named Onesimus who is the subject of this epistle (vv. 8-16). Onesimus ran away from Philemon. While Paul was imprisoned at Rome, he converted Onesimus (v. 10). Although Onesimus was helpful to Paul in Rome, he was still Philemon's property and needed to be returned to him (vv. 11-14).

Under Roman law, a master could punish a runaway slave any way he saw fit, including putting him to death. This short epistle was Paul's heartfelt appeal for Philemon to do the right thing regarding Onesimus (vv. 8-21). He had treated other Christians in a commendable manner (vv. 4-7); now he must do the same for Onesimus.

Spotlight

Do the right thing.

Having **confidence** in your **obedience**, I write to you, knowing that you will **do** even **more** than I say.

- Philemon 21

QUESTIONS

14. Explain why Paul wrote this letter to Philemon. ____________________

____

____

15. What did Paul mean when he said that he had "begotten" Onesimus (v. 10)? ____________________

____

____

16. What confidence did Paul have in Philemon (v. 21)? ____________________

____

____

Lesson 8

First and Second Thessalonians

Highlights

God teaches us to love one another (1 Thessalonians 4:9-10).

The resurrection of the dead (1 Thessalonians 4:13-18).

The Lord's second coming (1 Thessalonians 5:1-4).

Retribution at the Lord's return (2 Thessalonians 1:6-10).

Withdrawing from every brother who walks disorderly (2 Thessalonians 3:6-15).

Author

Paul authored these epistles.

Date

First Thessalonians was probably written between 50-52 AD while Paul was at Corinth on his second missionary journey. Second Thessalonians was probably written from Corinth a few months after the first epistle.

Purpose

Paul wrote these epistles to encourage a young church to faithfully endure persecution and to be ready for the Lord's return.

Paul visited Thessalonica on his second missionary journey. He established a congregation full of excited converts, many of whom were Gentiles. Envious Jews in Thessalonica stirred up violent persecution against these Christians. Under the cover of darkness, they evacuated Paul and his companions, but this young congregation remained and persevered in a city full of opposition (Acts 17:1-10).

Spotlight

Be ready when Jesus comes again.

For what is our **hope**, or **joy**, or crown of **rejoicing**? Is it not even **you** in the presence of our **Lord** Jesus Christ at His **coming**?

- 1 Thessalonians 2:19

Paul was concerned about the Christians he had left behind. From Athens, he sent Timothy back to Thessalonica to encourage them and bring him a report of their status (1 Thessalonians 3:1-7). He was relieved to hear they were maintaining their faith and serving the Lord.

Timothy also brought back a question they had regarding Christ's second coming. In this epistle, Paul gave detailed instructions regarding this subject.

FIRST THESSALONIANS

Their Great Example (Chapter 1)

Paul began the epistle by mentioning his continuing prayer for them. He clung to his fond memories of their ceaseless faith, effectual love, and enduring hope. They had responded to Paul's powerful preaching and became followers of the Lord despite the affliction and persecution they endured (vv. 2-6).

Their reception of the gospel was so impressive that it became an example for others to follow. Word of their conversion had spread to the extent that people were telling Paul the story of how he had won the Thessalonians to Christ. Note how Paul described their conversion. They had turned to God from their religious error, they were serving God and they were living in hope awaiting the coming of Christ (vv. 9-10).

QUESTIONS

1. What three things did Paul remember about the Thessalonians (1:3)?

    ____

    ____

    ____

2. What had the Thessalonians become to other believers (v. 7)?__________

    ____

    ____

3. How did Paul describe their conversion (vv. 9-10)?__________

    ____

    ____

Paul's Relationship to the Thessalonians (Chapters 2-3)

Paul reminded them of his character and conduct while he was among them. The preaching done by Paul and his companions, Silas and Timothy, did not contain error or deceit. They did not use flattering words to fleece them of their money. They did not seek glory from men; nor did they impose their apostolic authority upon them.

Paul said they were gentle among them as a mother caring for her young. They had given themselves entirely to the Thessalonians, working with their own hands to support themselves financially so as not to burden them. In both instruction and example, they exhorted the Thessalonians to walk worthy of God (vv. 1-12).

Paul commended these Christians for receiving his preaching as the true word of God and continuing in its teaching despite suffering persecution from the unbelievers in their city. Having been forced to leave them before he wanted, Paul desired to return to see them, but he was hindered from doing so (vv. 13-20).

He had warned them that they would suffer persecution because of their faith. Satan takes advantage of weak and struggling Christians, tempting them to depart from the faith. Paul sent Timothy to strengthen and encourage them to remain faithful to the Lord (3:1-5).

Timothy returned with a favorable report of their faith and love. This news gave Paul great comfort and joy. His work among them had not been in vain. However, they still had work to do in order to be found blameless at the Lord's return (vv. 6-13).

QUESTIONS

4. How did the Thessalonians receive Paul's preaching (2:17)? ____________

____

____

5. Describe some of the persecution suffered by the Thessalonians that is recorded in the book of Acts (Acts 17:5-9). ____________________

____

____

____

The Call to Godly Living (4:1-12)

Like all large Gentile cities, Thessalonica contained idol temples and other opportunities to indulge in fleshly lusts. Christians must not pursue sinful desires, regardless of their surroundings. The Thessalonians had to abstain from sexual immorality and conduct themselves as godly and honorable people. The same instructions apply in today's world. Opportunities to engage in sexual sins abound in our society, but the Lord expects us to practice self-control and abstain from such sins (vv. 1-8).

These Christians excelled at practicing brotherly love. However, Paul exhorted them to increase in this great virtue. He also called on them to live quiet, peaceful, productive lives so they would set good examples for unbelievers (vv. 9-12).

QUESTIONS

6. From what sin were the Thessalonians to abstain (4:3)? ______________

    ____

7. What did Paul mean when he said, "that each of you should know how to possess his own vessel in sanctification and honor" (v. 4)? __________

    ____

    ____

    ____

8. What instruction did Paul give them concerning their love for one another (v. 10)?______________________________

    ____

    ____

9. What did Paul tell them regarding how to conduct themselves (v. 11)?

    ____

    ____

    ____

The Resurrection of the Dead (4:13-18)

The Thessalonians were troubled over a serious matter. They feared their brethren who had died would miss out on the glories of the Lord's return. Paul comforted these fears by assuring them their loved ones would not miss anything.

The first thing that will happen when the Lord descends from heaven is the resurrection of the dead. Then those who are alive will be caught up together with them to meet the Lord in the air. When Paul said, "and thus we shall always be with the Lord" (v. 17b), he meant both the living and the dead. These words comforted the Thessalonians, and they continue to comfort today's believers.

Preparation for the Lord's Return (5:1-11)

Comforting words were not to cause them to be careless about the Lord's second coming. Paul admonished the Thessalonians to be watchful and sober. They had been taught that the day of the Lord would come as a thief in the night. This was a part of the Lord's own teaching (Matthew 24:42-44; c.f. 2 Peter 3:10). This event will occur at an unexpected time. Those who are not prepared will miss out on the glories of the Lord's return. They needed comfort regarding those Christians who had already died, but they also needed exhortation about living so they would obtain their own salvation on that great day.

QUESTIONS

10. To whom was Paul referring when he spoke of "those who have fallen asleep" (4:13)? ____________________

    ____

11. What hope did Paul give the Thessalonians concerning these brethren?

    ____

    ____

    ____

12. Describe the events that will take place when the Lord returns (vv. 16-17). ____________________

    ____

    ____

    ____

13. What did Paul mean when he said, "the day of the Lord so comes as a thief in the night" (5:2)? ____________________

    ____

Closing Exhortations (5:12-28)

This epistle closes with one of Paul's lists of various exhortations. They were to:

- Honor and esteem their elders (vv. 12-13).
- Treat one another properly (vv. 14-15).
- Rejoice, pray, and give thanks always (vv. 16-18).
- Refrain from silencing those who were teaching them God's word (vv. 19-20).
- Test all things; hold fast what is good; abstain from every form of evil (vv. 21-22).

SECOND THESSALONIANS

Some of the Thessalonians had come to believe the Lord's return was eminent. This misunderstanding led them to stop working and become busybodies. False beliefs have consequences; they lead to sinful actions. Also, it appears that the persecution had grown worse since the first letter. Paul wrote Second Thessalonians to address these issues.

Judgment and Rest When the Lord Returns (Chapter 1)

Suffering for our faith can be discouraging, especially if nothing happens to those who cause our suffering. We have assurance that God will not allow such injustices to go unpunished. While the Lord's return will be a day of victory for the saved (1 Thessalonians 4:13-18), it will be a day of tribulation, fiery vengeance, and everlasting destruction for those who have opposed God. When the Lord is revealed, the persecuted saints will finally have rest and vindication.

Apostasy and the Man of Sin (Chapter 2)

The Thessalonians were not to allow themselves to be deceived regarding Christ's return. While no one could know the day, one thing had to happen prior to His coming. Paul said there would be a falling away, and the man of sin would be revealed (v. 3).

There continues to be much speculation regarding the identity of this "man of sin." Paul said that he would be unashamedly arrogant and be willing to be identified and worshiped as God. He was being restrained, but when Paul wrote this epistle, he was already at work, deceiving those who did not love and believe the truth (vv. 4-12).

The Thessalonians were to stand fast and hold on to the teachings they had received from Paul, whether in person or through writing. God would comfort their hearts and establish them in every good word and work (vv. 13-17).

Therefore, brethren, **stand fast** and hold the **traditions** which you were taught, whether by **word** or our **epistle**.

- 2 Thessalonians 2:15

Withdrawal from Those Walking Disorderly (Chapter 3)

Paul requested their prayers for him, that the gospel would have the same success in other places that it had among them. The Lord would establish them and guard them from the evil one. He also expressed confidence that they would do the things he had commanded (vv. 1-5).

There was a matter that needed their attention. Some among them were walking disorderly. Paul had told them "to lead a quiet life, to mind your own business, and to work with your own hands" (1 Thessalonians 4:11). While he was with them, he set an example of working with his own hands to support himself, and he commanded, "If anyone will not work, neither shall he eat" (2 Thessalonians 3:10). In spite of this, some among them were not obeying this command. They had stopped working and had become busybodies.

Paul commanded the faithful brethren to mark these individuals and withdraw from them. They were to stop recognizing them as faithful members of the church and refrain from social interaction with them. This would cause them to be ashamed of their conduct and repent. They were not to treat them as enemies but admonish them to correct their behavior.

QUESTIONS

14. When the Lord returns, what will happen to the enemies of God's people (1:6-9)? ______________________________

____

____

15. What two things are we to do with the truth (2:10, 12)? ______________

____

____

16. What medium does God use to *call* us to salvation (2:14)? ______________

____

____

17. Explain what is to be done to those who walk disorderly (3:6, 14-15)?

____

____

____

The Thessalonian epistles show us that a congregation can serve the Lord faithfully in the face of opposition if the members will love one another, live godly lives, and remain focused on their hope for the Lord's return.

Lesson 9

First and Second Timothy and Titus

Highlights

The church is the pillar and ground of the truth (1 Timothy 3:15).

"Let no one despise your youth" (1 Timothy 4:12).

"The love of money is a root of all kinds of evil" (1 Timothy 6:9-10).

"All Scripture is given by inspiration of God" (2 Timothy 3:16-17).

"Preach the word!" (2 Timothy 4:1-5).

Qualifications of elders and deacons (1 Timothy 3:1-13; Titus 1:5-9).

Author

Paul authored these epistles.

Date

First Timothy and Titus were probably written 64-65 AD.

Second Timothy was written shortly before Paul's death, probably 67-68 AD.

Purpose

Paul wrote these epistles to encourage two young men to fulfill the responsibilities of gospel preachers.

- *First Timothy* reminds the young evangelist how the local church should function and to fulfill his role as an evangelist (1 Timothy 3:14-15).

Spotlight

Guard the faith; preach the word!

Preach the word! Be ready **in** season and **out** of season. **Convince**, **rebuke**, **exhort**, with all **longsuffering** and **teaching**.

- 2 Timothy 4:2

- *Second Timothy* contains Paul's final words to Timothy. It provides a very personal look Paul's heart and mind just prior to his death.
- *Titus* encourages the young evangelist as he labors in the gospel on the island of Crete. Its contents are similar to the instructions found in First Timothy.

These epistles contain instructions and encouragement for preachers. As such, they are special books for today's preachers but should be studied by all Christians.

Because the instructions in First Timothy and Titus are similar, this lesson incorporates some passages from Titus as we study through First Timothy; then we will study Second Timothy.

Remain in Ephesus that you may **charge** some that they teach no other **doctrine**, nor give heed to **fables** and endless **genealogies**, which cause **disputes** rather than godly **edification** which is in **faith**.

- 1 Timothy 1:3b-4

FIRST TIMOTHY

The Charge to Stop False Doctrine (Chapter 1)

Paul previously left Timothy in Ephesus, where some were causing problems for the church. They were trying to be teachers but had no business teaching. The purpose of teaching in the local church is to build up and edify the members, but these individuals were causing disputes and speculation rather than edification.

The Lord's church is not an open forum where any idea can be taught and considered. Only the truth of God's word is to be taught in the church. The mouths of those who would teach or speak otherwise must be stopped (vv. 1-7; Titus 1:10-16). This is a difficult task, but Paul reminded Timothy that he was up to it. He was to wage the good warfare and protect his faith and good conscience, knowing that a neglected conscience can suffer shipwreck (vv. 18-20).

QUESTIONS

1. Why had Paul left Timothy in Ephesus (1:3)? ____________________

2. Can anyone be allowed to speak or teach whatever they want in the Lord's church? Why or why not? ____________________

3. What was Paul's opinion of himself before he became a Christian (vv. 13-15)? ____________________

Roles of Men and Women in the Local Church (Chapter 2)

Holy, peaceful and faithful men are to lead the prayers in the assemblies (vv. 1-8). These prayers are to be offered for all. We are to pray for our civic leaders that we may live in peace so the gospel can spread and save more people.

Women are to be submissive during the assemblies. They are to dress modestly and learn in respectful silence and submission. Women are not permitted to usurp authority over the men. God assigned this role because of the order of creation and the curse He placed on Eve (Genesis 3:16). Each gender is to respect the role given by God (vv. 9-15; Titus 2:1-8).

QUESTIONS

4. Why are we to pray for our civic leaders (vv. 1-4)? ____________________

5. What kind of men are to lead prayers in the worship assemblies (v. 8)? ____________________

6. Explain why women are not to teach or take the lead in the worship assemblies (vv. 11-15). ____________________

Qualifications of Elders and Deacons (Chapter 3)

In His wisdom, God has designed the local church to be overseen by elders and served by deacons. Not just any person can serve in these positions. Elders, deacons and their wives must meet specific qualifications (vv. 1-13; Titus 1:5-9).

QUESTIONS

7. When do you think a man needs to begin developing his qualifications to serve as a deacon or elder? ______________________________

____

8. Which qualification to be an elder stands out to you as being most important? Why?______________________________

____

____

____

9. What are the qualifications for the wives of elders and deacons (v. 11)?

____

____

____

____

Responsibilities and Character of Preachers (Chapter 4)

Paul warned Timothy of the certainty of a coming apostasy. Some would depart from the faith, speaking lies and forbidding Christians to marry or to eat certain foods (vv. 1-5).

He counseled Timothy to respond to this danger by giving heed to himself and his work. He must discipline himself so he would be fit for this challenge (vv. 6-11). Staying spiritually fit is more important than staying physically fit.

Timothy received various charges related to his work.

- Command and teach the words of faith and doctrine (v. 11).
- Be a good example to the believers (v. 12).
- Give attention to reading, exhorting and teaching (v. 13).
- Do not neglect the gift given to him (v. 14).

- Give himself entirely to his task (v. 15).
- Take heed to himself and his teaching (v. 16).

QUESTIONS

10. Explain why godliness is more profitable than bodily exercise (v. 8).

____

____

11. How was Timothy to overcome prejudice associated with his youth (v. 12)?

____

____

____

12. Does this apply only to preachers, or should all young Christians follow these instructions? ____________________

Treatment of Church Members (Chapter 5)

The preacher must be careful to maintain proper relationships with all the church members (vv. 1-2). He must show respect for older members and treat younger members as brothers and sisters.

The local church is responsible for caring for members who are in financial need (vv. 3-16). Paul gave strict regulations regarding when a widow is to be cared for by the local church. These verses also provide good instructions regarding how Christians are to care for their family members (vv. 4, 8, 16).

Preachers have a special relationship with the elders of the local congregation (vv. 17-25). Elders who serve well are to be honored. Only serious accusations against elders are to be considered. If an elder is sinning, he is to be rebuked before the entire church. Timothy was to ensure that he did this carefully and without partiality.

QUESTIONS

13. How was Timothy to treat older members of the church (vv. 1-2)? ______

____

____

14. How was he to treat younger members of the church? ____________

____

____

15. What did Paul say about Christians who would not provide for their own households (v. 8)? ____________________

____

____

16. What principle did Timothy have to follow when correcting those in sin (v. 21)? ____________________

____

____

Exhortations to Timothy and Various Groups (Chapter 6)

This epistle's final chapter contains instructions for Timothy and for various individuals in the local church.

- Slaves are to honor and serve their masters (vv. 1-2).
- The church is to withdraw from false teachers (vv. 3-5).
- Those who desire to be rich are in danger (vv. 6-10).
- Timothy was to flee covetousness, pursue the right things, fight the good fight of faith—and do so blamelessly (vv. 11-16).
- The rich are not to trust in their wealth; they are to share it with others (vv. 17-19).
- Timothy was to guard what was placed in his trust and avoid those things that could destroy both his work and his personal faith (vv. 20-21).

QUESTIONS

17. Why will those who desire to be rich fall into temptations and a snare (vv. 9-10)? ____________________

____

____

18. What instructions did Paul give to the rich (vv. 17-19)? ____________________

____

____

SECOND TIMOTHY

This letter contains Paul's final words to Timothy. It is an urgent, heartfelt summons for Timothy to come to Rome where Paul is awaiting his execution. Although Paul hoped to see Timothy in person before his death, the letter expressed many of the things he wanted Timothy to know.

A new danger was facing Christians. Rome burned in 64 A.D. The emperor Nero blamed the Christians. Across the empire, Christian leaders were being arrested and brought to Rome for trial and execution. Paul wrote to encourage Timothy as he faced this new persecution.

Be Courageous (1:1-12)

Paul reminded Timothy of the strong heritage of faith he had received from his grandmother and mother. God has not given us a spirit of fear, but of power, love, and a sound mind. Timothy was not to be ashamed of the gospel, or of those who were suffering for the gospel; rather, he should step forward and be willing to endure suffering for the cause of Christ.

Hold Fast the Pattern of Sound Words (1:13-18)

Timothy could endure these hard times by holding fast to the things he had been taught. The teachings of the Lord and His apostles constitute a pattern to follow. The Greek word for pattern refers to a detailed model to follow without deviation. These teachings are sound words to which we must hold fast (grip, cling to) and not let go.

QUESTIONS

19. What role had Timothy's mother and grandmother played in his spiritual development (1:5; 3:15)? ______________________________

____

____

20. To what was Timothy to hold fast (v. 13)? ______________________

____

Remain Prepared and Useful to the Lord (Chapter 2)

The Lord assigned several important responsibilities to preachers.

- Preachers must diligently equip themselves by studying the Scriptures (v. 15).
- Preachers must teach and equip others to teach God's word (v. 2).
- Like soldiers, preachers must give undivided attention to serving the Lord (vs. 3-4).

- Like athletes, preachers must follow the rules (v. 5).
- Preachers must be gentle and patient as they work to rescue those who are trapped in sin and error (vv. 24-26).

Paul also warned Timothy to shun profane and idle babblings (v. 16), to flee youthful lusts (v. 22), and to avoid foolish and ignorant disputes (v. 23).

QUESTIONS

21. Of the various responsibilities given to preachers in this chapter, which do you think would be the most difficult? Why? ____________________

____

____

____

____

Preach the Word of God (3:1-4:5)

Paul warned Timothy of difficulties that would come, not only from unbelievers, but also from some who had a form of godliness but were not truly following the Lord. Timothy was to turn away from such people (v. 5).

To sustain himself during these difficult times, Timothy had to adhere to God's Word. He was to carefully follow the teaching and example he received from Paul (vv. 10-11, 14). Paul reminded him that all Scripture was inspired by God and would equip him to do his important work (vs. 16-17).

Above all things, Timothy was to preach the word. He had to grow tired of convincing, rebuking, and exhorting. Some would not endure sound doctrine, but would turn to teachers who tickled their ears. Timothy had to be watchful in all things, endure affliction, do the work of an evangelist and fulfill his ministry.

QUESTIONS

22. What is the source of all Scripture (3:16)?____________________

____

____

23. What is Scripture able to accomplish (3:17)?____________________

____

____

24. What important task is given to preachers (4:2)? ______________________

____

____

Paul's Closing Remarks (4:6-22)

Paul knew his life was about to end. He had fought the good fight, finished the race and kept the faith. He was ready to receive the crown of righteousness (vv. 6-8).

Paul requested that Timothy come to him quickly (v. 9). Only Luke was with him (v. 11). Timothy was to bring Mark, Paul's cloak and his books and parchments (vs. 11, 13); and he urged Timothy to come before winter (v. 21).

QUESTIONS

25. What blessing awaits all Christians who fight the good fight, finish the race and keep the faith (vv. 7-8)? ______________________

____

____

____

Lesson 10

Hebrews

Highlights

The word of God is living and powerful, sharper than any two-edged sword (4:12).

Jesus is the author of salvation to all who obey Him (5:9).

Hope is the anchor of the soul (6:19).

"It is appointed for men to die once, but after this the judgment" (9:27).

"Not forsaking the assembling of ourselves together" (10:25).

The great chapter on faith (chapter 11).

Author

The author of this epistle is not identified. Many believe the apostle Paul wrote Hebrews.

Date

Uncertain, perhaps between 64-68 A.D.

Purpose

To stop Jewish Christians from abandoning the gospel and returning to the Law of Moses.

Although the specific recipients are not identified, it is clear this epistle was written to Christians who had been converted from Judaism. The writer quotes from the Old Testament and speaks in detail about religious practices under the Law of Moses. He also speaks of the recipients as having enjoyed the blessings and privileges of these

Spotlight

Christ is better.

But now He has obtained a more excellent **ministry**, inasmuch as He is also **Mediator** of a better **covenant**, which was established on better **promises**.

- Hebrews 8:6

practices. Because of Jesus Christ, these Jewish Christians were now under a better covenant (7:22), mediated by a better High Priest, based upon better promises (8:6) and obtained with a better sacrifice (9:23).

The epistle indicates that these Christians were suffering because of their faith in Christ. Over time, such persecution would have become a discouragement and pressured them to return to the old religious beliefs and practices with which they were more familiar. Doing so might relieve their suffering, but it would also condemn their souls.

The writer sets forth a series of logical arguments emphasizing the fact that the blessings obtained in Christ are far superior to those offered under the Law of Moses. He has interspersed these arguments with stern warnings against departing from the Gospel and returning to the Law of Moses. Doing so would cause them to lose their salvation.

This epistle relies heavily on the Old Testament. The writer directly quotes from the Old Testament about 35 times. He builds his arguments on the themes of the priesthood, the tabernacle and Israel entering the land of rest. These Old Testament themes are revealed to be types and shadows of real blessings found in Jesus Christ.

Christ is a Better Messenger (Chapters 1-2)

The epistle begins by acknowledging that, in times past, God spoke through messengers who would have been respected by these readers (1:1-2). However, in this dispensation (these last days), God speaks to us through His Son. His credentials make Him far superior to any prophet or even the angels.

Those who transgressed the Law of Moses were punished. Those who reject the message of salvation delivered by a superior Messenger will receive an even greater punishment (2:1-4).

Therefore we must give the more **earnest** heed to the things we have **heard**, lest we **drift away**.

- Hebrews 2:1

Although He was in heaven with the Father, Jesus voluntarily came to this earth to experience suffering and death for us. This enabled Him to destroy the devil's power. It also allowed Him to experience our kinds of struggles firsthand, thereby making Him a more merciful and faithful High Priest (vv. 9-18).

QUESTIONS

1. Why was the book of Hebrews written? ______________________________
____
____
____

2. By Whom does God speak to us in these last days (1:2)? ______________
____
____

3. What makes Jesus superior to any prophet or angel (vv. 2-3)? __________
____
____
____

4. What will happen to those who reject this superior Spokesman (2:1-4)?
____
____
____

Christ Gives Us a Better Hope (3:1-4:13)

Jesus is presented as being greater than Moses. This was an important point to make to these Jewish Christians. Moses led the Israelites to the Promised Land, but because of their unbelief most of them did not enter (3:7-19). The writer warned these Hebrew Christians they were capable of the same fatal unbelief manifested by their ancestors. Instead, they must hold fast to their faith and be steadfast until the end (vv. 12-14).

A glorious rest remains for the people of God, but to enter that rest we must be diligent and remain faithful (4:11). We can't fool God. He recognizes unbelief and disobedience. His Word can convict our hearts (v. 12). We will give account to an all-knowing God (v. 13).

QUESTIONS

5. Why did the Israelites who left Egypt fail to enter the Promised Land (3:12-13, 19)? ______

6. How is God's word described in Hebrews 4:12? ______

Christ is a Better High Priest (4:14-7:28)

The Jews depended on the High Priest to mediate before God on their behalf. Jesus is the Christian's High Priest. He is in heaven in God's presence interceding on our behalf (4:14-16).

The High Priests under the Law of Moses shared the weaknesses and imperfections common to man. They had to offer sacrifices for their own sins, and they were subject to death (5:1-4).

The writer wanted to speak of Jesus as a better High Priest, but before he did, he saw the need to rebuke these Christians for their spiritual immaturity (5:12-14). They needed to grow in their understanding of God's Word and of their faith in His promises (chapter 6).

Jesus was not made our High Priest according to the Law of Moses. Under that law, only men from the tribe of Levi could serve as priests. The fact that Jesus is serving as our High Priest means the law has changed (7:12). This is an important detail in the writer's argument.

Christ's priesthood is better because it is eternal and unchangeable (v. 24). He always lives to make intercession for us (v. 25). He is a perfect, sinless High Priest (vv. 26-28).

QUESTIONS

7. Explain how Jesus is a merciful, faithful, and sympathetic High Priest (2:17-18; 4:15). ______

8. What rebuke is given in Hebrews 5:12-14? ______

9. Explain how Jesus (Who was from the tribe of Judah) can serve as our High Priest. What has happened to the Law of Moses (7:12, 18)? ________

____

____

____

____

Jesus Offers a Better Covenant, Sanctuary, and Sacrifice (8:1-10:18)

The Law of Moses was never meant to be a permanent covenant. It served an important, but temporary, purpose. The writer quoted Jeremiah 31:31-34 to show that God always planned to replace the covenant He made through Moses with a better one (8:8-12). The covenant then being followed by the Jews was obsolete, growing old, and vanishing away (v. 13).

Chapter 9 contrasts the High Priest's service in the earthly sanctuary with that of Jesus in the heavenly sanctuary. The High Priest carefully followed the instructions given by Moses, and offered sacrifices for sins, but these sacrifices could never make man perfect or allow him to enter into God's presence.

Jesus offered His own blood once for all time, for all people. His death accomplished great things that could never be accomplished under the Law of Moses.

- It obtained our eternal redemption (v. 12).
- It cleansed our consciences from dead works to serve the living God (v. 14).
- It made Him the Mediator of the new covenant and allowed us to receive the promise of an eternal inheritance (v. 15).
- It brought the New Covenant into effect (vv. 16-17).

The blood of bulls and goats could not take away sins (10:4). A man, not an animal, was lost in the Garden of Eden. We had to be redeemed with a man's blood, not the blood of an animal. Jesus willingly came into this world and took on a physical body to offer as atonement for our sins (vv. 5-10).

QUESTIONS

10. What had God promised to make with the house of Israel and with the house of Judah (8:8)? ________

____

____

11. What was offered to obtain our eternal redemption (9:12-15)? ____

12. What must take place in order for us to receive remission of our sins (9:22)? ____

13. What cannot take away our sins (10:4)? ____

14. What did Jesus voluntarily do to atone for our sins (10:5-10)? ____

Exhortations to Faithfulness and Perseverance (10:19-12:29)

Because of everything Jesus did for us, through His blood, we are able to enter God's presence with confidence. We are to hold fast to our hope without wavering and encourage one another to remain faithful (10:19-25).

Willfully walking away from the gospel will surely bring God's wrath. These Christians had already endured struggles and sufferings. They must not quit now. They needed endurance to finish the course and receive the promise (vv. 26-39).

These Hebrew Christians needed to be reminded of their heritage. They were descended from men and women of great faith. Chapter 11 sets forth the faithfulness, obedience, and endurance of Abel, Enoch, Noah, Abraham and Sarah, Moses, Joshua, Rahab, the judges, David and the prophets as examples for them to follow.

Jesus presented the greatest example of obedience and endurance. He endured the cross. We have not experienced the sufferings He endured (12:1-4).

The writer admonished his readers to view their suffering as discipline from God (vv. 5-11). They were to strengthen one another, knowing they were coming into God's kingdom and presence. They must be careful to serve God acceptably, with reverence and godly fear (vv. 12-29).

QUESTIONS

15. What is to take place when Christians assemble together (10:24-25)?

16. What is faith (11:1)?

17. Choose one person mentioned in chapter 11. Tell what their faith caused them to do and how this was rewarded by God.

18. What two things are we to pursue (12:14)? Why?

Concluding Exhortations and Prayer (Chapter 13)

The epistle concludes with various instructions, like those found in other epistles, regarding holy living and faithfulness. They are not to allow themselves to be carried about with strange doctrines. They must be willing to suffer and bear the reproach of Christ (13:1-17).

The writer closes by requesting their prayers and blessing them.

QUESTIONS

19. What is to continue (13:1)?

20. What promise from God allows us to be content with our physical blessings (vv. 5-6)?

21. What are we to offer unto God (v. 15)? ____________________

____

____

22. What other sacrifices please God (v. 16)? ____________________

____

____

While we may not be tempted to return to the Law of Moses, we can be tempted to abandon our faith for various other reasons. The book of Hebrews warns us of the spiritual danger in which we place ourselves if we fall into any kind of apostasy. What we have obtained in Christ is better than anything else we will ever find. Like those who have served God before us, let's live faithful and strive to enter our eternal rest.

Lesson 11

James

Highlights

"Be doers of the word, and not hearers only" (1:22).

Faith and works (2:14-26).

Taming the tongue (3:1-12).

"Draw near to God and He will draw near to you" (4:8).

"The effective, fervent prayer of a righteous man avails much" (5:16).

Author

The author of this epistle is identified as James. There are several men in the New Testament who have this name. We don't know for sure who this James was, but many believe it was the Lord's brother.

Date

Uncertain, as early as 42 A.D. or as late as 65 A.D.

Purpose

To help God's people develop and practice "pure and undefiled religion."

The book of James is one of the easiest books of the Bible to read and understand. It does not address complicated problems or doctrinal issues. It contains practical instructions for applying the gospel to the daily life of the child of God. This book has been called "The Christian's Book of Proverbs" and "The Gospel of Common Sense." James shows us how to take our religion with us when we leave the church building.

Spotlight

Practical Christianity.

Pure and **undefiled** religion before God and the Father is this: to visit **orphans** and **widows** in their **trouble**, and to keep oneself **unspotted** from the **world**.

- James 1:27

The consistent theme throughout the book of James is genuineness. It is an appeal to the Lord's people to seriously consider whether or not they are living as true disciples should.

James is a general epistle, which means it is not written to a specific congregation or individual but is meant to be circulated and read by many Christians. The challenges being addressed in the epistle are those that all believers face.

Facing Trials and Temptations (1:1-20)

James began his epistle by addressing something common to every person—enduring trials and suffering. He said we must look upon such occasions with joy, not because they are pleasant to experience, but because of what they can accomplish. Enduring trials with the right attitude results in further development of character (vv. 2-4).

To help us have this proper attitude and understanding, we are encouraged to pray for wisdom. However, we must pray in faith with no doubting. One who doubts is unstable and should not expect to receive anything from the Lord (vv. 5-8).

Blessed is the man who endures **temptation**; for when he has been **approved**, he will receive the **crown** of life which the Lord has **promised** to those who **love** Him.

- James 1:12

Instead of trusting in ourselves, we must learn to trust in God to see us through times of suffering (vv. 9-11).

Christians must endure temptations to sin (vv. 12-18). Temptations come from Satan. He appeals to our desires and entices us to fulfill them in ways that violate God's will. When we do so, we sin and bring spiritual death upon ourselves. God does not tempt us to sin. He gives us good things, and causes us to have spiritual life, not death.

We endure times of trials and temptations by being patient, not by lashing out or giving up. We must be quick to hear, slow to speak, and slow to wrath (vv. 19-20).

QUESTIONS

1. How are we to react to trials and suffering? Why (vv. 2-4)?____________

2. What has God promised to give us if we ask for it (v. 5)? ____________

3. How does James describe the person who has no faith (vv. 6-8)? ______

4. Identify the three avenues through which Satan tempts us to sin (1 John 2:16). ____________

5. God does not tempt us to sin, but what does He do to help us with temptations (1 Corinthians 10:13)? ____________

Being Doers of the Word (1:21-27)

The Christian is saved by God's Word, but only if he receives it in the proper manner. Like a man clearing off ground to plant a garden, I must clear the sin from my heart and receive God's word with meekness (v. 21).

However, receiving the Word is not enough. We must be doers of the Word and not hearers only (v. 22). The person who only hears the Word will quickly lose it (Luke 8:12). He must listen with a mind to obey.

James describes a person who looks at himself in the mirror, sees his reflection, but walks away and immediately forgets that he needs to correct his appearance. Merely seeing his reflection did not help him. Likewise, just hearing God's Word without making needed corrections does not really help us. The one who continues in active obedience will be blessed (vv. 23-25).

Pure and undefiled religion is not possessed by one who merely hears the word. It is seen in one who practices self-control and helps those who are in need (vv. 26-27).

QUESTIONS

6. What must we clear away from our hearts before we can receive God's Word (v. 21)? ____
____
____

7. What attitude does one need to successfully receive God's Word (v. 21)?
____
____

8. How does James describe one who hears the Word but does not act upon it (vv. 23-25)? ____
____
____

9. How does one show pure and undefiled religion (vv. 26-27)?__________
____
____
____

Respect of Persons (2:1-13)

Practicing prejudice and showing favoritism are unbecoming traits for any person, especially a Christian. James illustrates this by presenting a situation in which two visitors are treated differently based on their appearances (vv. 2-4). Such behavior reveals our evil thoughts and condemns us as transgressors. We are to love our neighbors as ourselves. Instead of showing favoritism to better ourselves, we must practice mercy toward all mankind.

Faith Without Works (2:14-26)

Christians are people of faith. We walk by faith. We are saved by faith. However, our faith must express itself in works of obedience.

Faith without works is dead. Such faith is unprofitable and cannot save us (v. 14). Abraham was a man of great faith, but his faith was not perfected and did not save him until it was expressed in obedience to God's command (vv. 21-23). Rahab was saved because she acted upon her belief. She expressed her faith in works (v. 25). One is justified by works, and not by faith only.

QUESTIONS

10. What do we reveal about ourselves when we mistreat people based on how they appear (v. 4)? ____________________

11. What is the royal law (v. 8)? ____________________

12. Why should we show mercy to others (vv. 12-13)? ____________________

13. What does James say about faith without works (vv. 17, 20, 26)? ____________________

14. When was Abraham's faith made perfect, thus justifying him before God (vv. 21-24)? ____________________

Dangers of the Tongue (3:1-12)

The Bible has a lot to say about the way we use our tongues. This makes sense. Everyone has one and uses it every day. Notice some of the practical points James made about our tongues.

- The ability to bridle and control the tongue is a mark of maturity (v. 2).
- The tongue is a small part of the body, but it has the power to do great things—both good and evil (vv. 3-4).
- The tongue is likened to a fire (vv. 5-6). If controlled, fire can accomplish good things. It can cook our food and provide heat and light. However, if allowed to get out of control, fire can do great harm.
- Man has been able to tame every kind of wild beast, but he struggles to tame his own tongue (vv. 7-8).
- Nature is consistent, but we can be shamefully inconsistent in the ways we use our tongues (vv. 9-12).

Wisdom (3:13-18)

Instead of seeking praise and admiration for our speech, we should be known for our wisdom. The way we treat others reveals whether we are following the world or God. Selfish and destructive behavior shows that we follow the wisdom of the world (vv. 14-16). Pure, peaceable, gentle, and merciful behavior proves we are following the wisdom from above (vv. 17-18).

QUESTIONS

15. How is the tongue like the bit put in a horse's mouth or the rudder on a ship (vv. 3-5)? ____________________

____

____

16. How is the tongue like a fire (vv. 5-6)?____________________

____

____

17. Explain why you think people have a hard time controlling their tongue.

____

____

____

____

18. How can we know that a person is following the wisdom of the world (vv. 14-16)? ____________________

____

____

19. Describe the wisdom that is from above (v. 17).____________________

____

____

Problems with Pride (Chapter 4)

Pride causes the greatest man-made sorrows the world faces. Wars and fights result when people seek their own will. The world has a strong pull on each of us. However, trying to be friends with the world will make us enemies of God, who jealously desires our full devotion. We must resist the devil's appeal to our pride, repent of our sins, and draw near to God (vv. 1-10).

Pride can cause us to speak against and mistreat our brethren (vv. 11-12). Pride can also cause us to forget about the uncertainty of life (vv. 13-17). We can get so caught up in making a successful life in this world that we forget about our responsibilities toward God. Instead of seeking our own will, we must seek God's will.

QUESTIONS

20. What happens when a Christian tries to be a friend of the world (v. 4)?

____

____

____

21. Describe ways a Christian might try to be a friend of the world. ________

____

____

____

22. What happens when we resist the devil (v. 7)? ______________________

____

____

23. How does James describe the uncertainty of physical life (v. 14)? _______

____

____

____

24. How does James describe sin in verse 17?________________________

____

____

____

Patience During Suffering (Chapter 5)

James shifts from talking about the suffering of others to enduring suffering caused by others. God will judge those who mistreat and abuse others (vv. 1-6). The faithful Christian must patiently endure unfair sufferings, knowing that God works things out in His own time (vv. 7-8).

Christians are not to turn on one another during times of suffering and uncertainty. We must commit ourselves to a God who has proven that He takes care of His own (vv. 9-12). We have the Old Testament accounts of the prophets and Job as examples of God's care for His people.

Instead of giving up on God and turning on one another, Christians are to pray, worship, and lean on one another through difficult times (vv. 13-15).

James' statement, "The effective, fervent prayer of a righteous man avails much," means that prayer works if we work it. The power of prayer is available to every child of God (vv. 16-18).

Sometimes Christians become weary in their suffering and depart from God. We have an obligation not to allow our brethren to give up when times are tough. We are to be there for them, encourage them and exhort them to remain faithful to the Lord (vv. 19-20).

QUESTIONS

25. What lesson are we to learn from a farmer (vv. 7-8)?________________

26. What lesson are we to learn from the prophets and Job (vv. 10-11)? ____

27. What must accompany our prayers in order for them to be answered (v. 15; 1:5)?________________

28. What responsibility do we have towards Christians who give up and walk away from the Lord (vv. 19-20)?________________

It is easy to become overwhelmed by the Bible's message. The epistle of James teaches us how to make practical use of our faith. The teachings of Jesus and His apostles aren't just for Sundays. They have an application in our daily lives. Let's be doers of the word and strive to have pure and undefiled religion.

Lesson 12

First and Second Peter and Jude

Highlights

"Be holy, for I am holy" (1 Peter 1:16).

Always be ready to give an answer (1 Peter 3:15).

The devil is like a roaring lion (1 Peter 5:8).

The Christian graces (2 Peter 1:5-7).

The Day of the Lord (2 Peter 3:10-13).

Contend earnestly for the faith (Jude 3).

Author

The apostle Peter authored First and Second Peter.

More than likely, the Lord's brother wrote Jude.

Date

First Peter was probably written in 64-65 A.D.

Second Peter and Jude were probably written in 66-67 A.D.

Recipients

"To the pilgrims of the Dispersion in Pontus, Galatia, Cappadocia, Asia, and Bithynia" (1 Peter 1:1; see 2 Peter 3:1). These were provinces in Asia Minor. These two epistles were intended for all the churches of Asia Minor. We include a study of Jude in this lesson because it is very similar to 2 Peter chapter two.

FIRST PETER

This epistle addresses the threat of suffering and persecution (1 Peter 4:12-13). When the Lord's

Spotlight

The suffering Christian.

Yet if anyone **suffers** as a **Christian**, let him not be **ashamed**, but let him **glorify God** in this matter.

- 1 Peter 4:16

church began, persecution came primarily from Jewish sources. However, during the reign of the Roman Emperor Nero, Christians, specifically, were accused and targeted as enemies of Rome. This brought a change to the lives of all Christians living in the Roman Empire. Where there had been peace and toleration, there would now be threats and persecution. Peter wrote this epistle to address these circumstances. He gave these Christians reasons to remain faithful during their suffering and practical instructions regarding how to live in the face of these sufferings.

Our Great Salvation (1:1-12)

Peter began his epistle by calling attention to their great salvation—the reason for their suffering. These Christians had a living hope (vv. 3-5). They needed to remember that, despite their temporary suffering, they had an incorruptible and undefiled inheritance reserved for them in Heaven.

The grievous trials they were facing served an important purpose—to strengthen their faith and bring about their salvation (vv. 6-9). The prophets, and even the angels of heaven, had shown great interest in this salvation (vv. 10-12). This blessing was too precious to forfeit because of temporary persecution.

Therefore **gird up** the loins of your **mind**, be **sober**, and rest your **hope** fully upon the **grace** that is to be brought to you at the **revelation** of Jesus Christ.

- 1 Peter 1:13

Called to Live Holy Lives (1:13-2:12)

Suffering does not excuse one from the obligation to live a holy life. We cannot be careless about the way we live (v. 13). Peter gave three good reasons why Christians should live sin-free lives.

- God is holy and has always called upon His people to be holy (vv. 15-16).
- God will judge us according to our deeds (v. 17).
- God redeemed us with His Son's shed blood (vv. 18-19).

Christians are expected to grow spiritually, increasing in our knowledge of God's Word (2:1-3).

We are saved for a purpose (vv. 4-10). While the world may despise and reject us, Christians are precious to, and chosen by, God. We are a spiritual house (His church) and a holy priesthood, built upon Jesus Christ, Who is the Chief Cornerstone, to offer spiritual sacrifices to God (v. 5). As God's own special people, we are a chosen generation, a royal priesthood and a holy nation.

We are not to live like those in the sinful world around us (vv. 11-12). We are to conduct ourselves honorably before unbelievers. Realizing that we are sojourners and pilgrims in this world, we are to abstain from fleshly lusts, which war against our souls.

QUESTIONS

1. How did Peter describe our inheritance (1:4)? ____________________
   ____
   ____

2. What two things work together to preserve this inheritance (1:5)? ______
   ____
   ____

3. Explain how temporary suffering would benefit their faith (1:7). ________
   ____
   ____
   ____

4. What three reasons did Peter give for living a holy life (1:15-19)? _______
   ____
   ____
   ____

5. How are Christians to conduct themselves in this world (2:11)? _______
   ____
   ____
   ____

Duties Toward Others (2:13-3:12)

Christians are to obey and honor governing authorities (vv. 13-17). Remember, much of their persecution was coming from governing authorities, but God still expected His people to be obedient and submissive. The only time we are allowed to disobey the government is when its commands call upon us to disobey God (Acts 5:29).

Peter told the Christians who were slaves to obey their masters (vv. 18-20), even if these masters were harsh and unreasonable.

Sometimes, when we go through difficult times, we antagonize those closest to us. Peter reminded husbands and wives of their responsibilities toward one another (3:1-7).

All Christians are to be united, compassionate, loving, tender and humble toward one another (vv. 8-12).

The Suffering Christian's Influence (3:13-4:19)

Suffering Christians may not think they are accomplishing anything significant for the Lord, but Peter emphasized that we influence others by the way we endure our suffering.

- When possible, we are to use our suffering as an opportunity to share the gospel with the lost. Be ready to give an answer to those who ask why you are remaining faithful during your suffering (3:15).
- Do not join the world in its sin but live according to God's commandments (4:1-6). This causes some to think you are strange, but it is better for the world to think you are strange than to have God judge you as being unrighteous.
- Be a source of encouragement to fellow believers (vv. 7-11). Pray for one another; love one another; extend hospitality; encourage one another; serve one another—all to God's glory.
- Rejoice in your suffering (vv. 12-18). It is an honor to partake of Christ's sufferings, knowing you will be glorified and vindicated when He is revealed.
- Commit your soul to God in doing good (v. 19). The world can only take our physical lives (Matthew 10:28). Trust God to save your soul.

QUESTIONS

6. Who gave us an example of how to endure unfair suffering (2:21)? ______

____

7. What must Christians always be ready to do (3:15)?______________

____

____

8. What kinds of things can we no longer do after we become Christians (4:3)?____

9. What are we to have for one another (4:8)?____

10. What are those who suffer according to the will of God supposed to do (4:19)? ____

Closing Exhortations (Chapter 5)

- Peter exhorted the elders to keep close watch over their flocks (vv. 1-4). These were difficult times. Their leadership would be very important.
- The younger Christians were to submit to the older; all were to submit to one another (v. 5).
- They were to humble themselves before God, casting their cares upon Him (vs. 6-7), while resisting the devil (vv. 8-9).
- They were to stand in the true grace of God (vv. 10-14).

QUESTIONS

11. Explain the responsibilities given to elders (5:1-3). ____

12. What does God invite us to do (5:7)?____

13. How did Peter describe the devil (5:8)? ____

14. How must Christians respond to his efforts to devour us (5:9)? ________

SECOND PETER

While First Peter addressed an external threat (suffering caused by persecution), Second Peter addressed an internal threat (false teachers and false teaching).

Make Your Call and Election Sure (Chapter 1)

Before exposing the false teachers, Peter encouraged the Christians to equip themselves to defend against false doctrine and false teachers. He admonished them to grow spiritually by diligently adding specific virtues to their faith (vv. 5-7).

Possessing these characteristics causes one to be fruitful; he will never stumble; and he will be supplied an entrance into the everlasting kingdom (vv. 8-11). Neglecting such essential qualities causes one to be spiritually blind and vulnerable to false teachers.

QUESTIONS

15. List the characteristics we are to add to our faith (1:5-7). ________

16. What happens to the Christian who fails to develop his faith (1:9)? ________

17. Why was Peter writing this epistle (1:12-13)? ________

18. What role did the Holy Spirit play in the writing of the Scriptures (1:21; cf. John 16:12-13; 1 Cor. 2:9-13)? ________

Destructive Doctrines and False Teachers (Chapter 2)

Peter warns of the certainty of false teachers (vv. 1-3). Such individuals are dangerous because many people follow them. God has always exercised judgment against those who teach and practice error (vv. 4-11).

Peter specifies the characteristics of these false teachers (vv. 12-17). They speak evil of things they don't understand, shamelessly sin before others, have eyes full of adultery, and hearts trained in covetousness. They are like clouds without rain—they promise but do not deliver.

They promise liberty to those who are already free from sin, but they themselves are actually slaves, returning to sin and leading others to do the same (vv. 18-22).

Christ's Second Coming (Chapter 3)

Peter mentions one specific error that was spreading through their midst—the idea that Jesus would not return to judge the world. Those spreading this error would scoff at these warnings, insisting that God wouldn't come to judge them. Their argument was that He hadn't intervened thus far, so it is certain that He never would (vv. 3-4).

Such individuals willingly forget the facts (vv. 5-7). This world is not eternal. It had a beginning. God had intervened to bring judgment in the past. He destroyed the world by water in Noah's day. He is currently preserving this same world to be destroyed by fire.

The passing of time does not negate God's promise (vv. 8-9). The passing of time is evidence of God's patience, not His indifference.

The Day of the Lord will come (vv. 10-13). It will come suddenly and unexpectedly, at which time this physical universe will be destroyed. This fact should motivate us to be faithful to God, not careless in our living.

Peter closes this epistle by admonishing them to diligently prepare for the Lord's coming. He commends Paul's writings as Scripture (vv. 15-16). Peter has forewarned and reminded them, lest they be led away by these false teachers (v. 17). They are to grow in their knowledge of the Lord (v. 18).

QUESTIONS

19. Explain why false teachers are so dangerous (2:1-2). ________________

____

____

____

20. What two graphic illustrations did Peter use to describe the spiritual condition of those who return to sin and error (2:20-22)? ____________

____

____

____

21. Why has the Lord delayed returning to judge the world (3:9)? ____________

____

____

22. What will happen to this physical world when the Lord returns (3:10-12)?

____

____

____

23. What was Peter's final admonition (3:18)? ____________

____

____

JUDE

This general epistle is written to warn against the dangers of false teachers who had crept into the church (v. 4). The teachings of this epistle are almost identical to 2 Peter chapter 2.

Jude exhorts his readers to "contend earnestly for the faith which was once for all delivered to the saints" (v. 3). We are not to be passive, but must actively defend the faith. It has been "once for all," one time for all time, delivered. This does away with all kinds of latter-day revelations, such as the Koran, the Book of Mormon, and the messages of so-called modern-day prophets.

Whereas Peter admonishes his readers to protect themselves, Jude adds another responsibility. Christians are to actively try to rescue and protect those who are being led away in the error of false teachers (vv. 20-23)

Conclusion

The instructions found in these epistles are good for Christians of all times. We will all be called upon to suffer in different ways during our lives. It is important to remember that Satan is behind all suffering. God has given us what we need to endure. We have the faith once for all delivered to the saints, and we have a living hope of an inheritance in heaven. And we have our brethren to help us.

Lesson 13

First, Second and Third John

Highlights

God is light (1 John 1:5); God is love (4:8); God is great (3:20).

"If we confess our sins, He is faithful and just to forgive us our sins and to cleanse us from all unrighteousness" (1 John 1:9).

The lust of the flesh, the lust of the eyes and the pride of life (1 John 2:16).

Sin is lawlessness (1 John 3:4); sin is unrighteousness (5:17).

"Beloved, do not believe every spirit, but test the spirits, whether they are of God; because many false prophets have gone out into the world" (1 John 4:1).

Author

The apostle John authored these epistles.

John's name does not appear in these letters. However, they are similar to the Gospel of John, and many statements by the early church writers accredit these letters to John.

Date

The exact dates of these epistles are uncertain, but they were likely written in the 90s A.D.

Uniting Theme

- The Bible doctrine of fellowship is an important theme in John's epistles. Fellowship means sharing together or joint participation.

Spotlight

Fellowship with God and His people.

That which we have **seen** and **heard** we **declare** to you, that you also may have **fellowship** with us; and truly our fellowship is with the **Father** and with His Son **Jesus Christ**.

- 1 John 1:3

But if we **walk** in the **light** as He is in the **light**, we have **fellowship** with one another, and the **blood** of Jesus Christ His Son **cleanses** us from all **sin**.

- 1 John 1:7

- Each Christian is blessed to have fellowship with God and with other Christians. However, this fellowship must be obtained and maintained on God's terms. We must walk in the light—walk in the truth set forth in God's Word (1 John 1:5-7). When we do, we have fellowship with God and with others who are also walking in the truth.
- Extending fellowship to one who is not in fellowship with God severs one's own fellowship with God (2 John 9-11).
- Denying fellowship to those who are in fellowship with God is evil and harms our fellowship with God (3 John 9-11).
- While there are other important themes in these epistles, we will use fellowship as the theme for our study in this lesson.

FIRST JOHN

Recipients

The recipients were not specified. This general epistle was written to all Christians. The initial recipients were probably the churches in Asia Minor.

Purpose

To warn against false doctrine (1 John 2:26; 5:13).

John said that many had arisen who were not teaching and practicing the truth (2:18-19; 4:1). He wrote this letter to expose the false teachers as well as to encourage and equip those who were standing in the truth.

The epistle of First John is not organized as neatly as other epistles. Instead of studying it chapter by chapter, we will do a topical study that draws attention to the characteristics of those with whom we may have fellowship.

Those Who Walk in the Light, Not in Darkness (1:1-2:6; 5:2-3)

John began his epistle by assuring his readers that he was more than just a witness of the facts concerning Jesus. He had heard, seen, examined, and even touched the Son of God. He was sharing these facts so they could have fellowship with other believers and with God (vv. 1-4).

God is light. He is perfect holiness, righteousness, and truth. There is no darkness in God. Fellowship with Him is possible only if we walk in and practice the truth. When we sin, we must confess our sins and seek God's forgiveness. Those who continue to live in sin do not have fellowship with God (vv. 5-10).

Our claim to "know" God (have fellowship with Him) is true only if we are keeping His commandments and living according to His teachings (2:3-6).

QUESTIONS

1. Define the word fellowship. ______________________________

   ____

   ____

   ____

2. Why can we trust John's testimony regarding Jesus (1:1)? ______________

   ____

   ____

3. John said that God is light (1:5). Explain what this means.______________

   ____

   ____

   ____

4. Describe the benefits of walking in the light with God (1:7)? ______________

   ____

   ____

   ____

5. What must Christians do to receive forgiveness of their sins (1:9; Acts 8:22)? ______________________________

   ____

   ____

   ____

Those Who Love Their Brethren (2:7-11; 3:11-23; 4:7-21)

Loving the brethren is an important theme in this epistle. The Lord gave His disciples a new commandment to follow. "A new commandment I give to you, that you love one another; as I have loved you, that you also love one another. By this all will know that you are My disciples, if you have love for one another" (John 13:34-35). John emphasized this command in his epistle. One who loves his brother is walking in the light. One who hates his brother is stumbling in spiritual darkness (2:7-11).

The one who hates his brother is a murderer. He may not actually shed blood, but murder begins with hatred in one's heart. Instead, we ought to follow Christ's example and be willing to lay down our lives for our brethren. If we are willing to make such an extreme sacrifice for our brethren, certainly we should be willing to share our belongings to relieve their needs (3:11-19).

God is love. He who does not love cannot claim to know (be in fellowship with) God. We must show this love towards our brethren. We cannot see God, but we do see our brethren (4:7-12). John asked, "for he who does not love his brother whom he has seen, how can he love God whom he has not seen? And this is the commandment we have from Him: that he who loves God must love his brother also" (4:20-21).

QUESTIONS

6. How does John describe one who hates his brother (2:9-11)? ____________

   ____

   ____

7. Explain why John says, "whoever hates his brother is a murderer" (3:15).

   ____

   ____

   ____

8. How should Christians react to the fact that Jesus laid down His life for them (3:16)? ____

   ____

   ____

9. John said that God is love (4:7-8). Explain what this means. ____________

   ____

   ____

   ____

10. Why should it be easier to love our fellowman than to love God (4:12, 20-21)? ____

____

____

Those Who Confess Jesus

The error addressed by John in this epistle is a false doctrine called Gnosticism. Gnostics held many complicated views that conflicted with Christianity. For instance, they claimed that God is pure and holy, while all physical matter is evil. They concluded that deity could not come into contact with physical matter. As a result, they insisted that Jesus either was not God's Son, or He did not have a physical body while on this earth. This explains why John made specific statements concerning one's confession regarding Jesus.

- *Confess Jesus is the Christ (2:18-23; 5:1).* The word "Christ" means "anointed one." This New Testament word corresponds to the Old Testament word "Messiah," the Deliverer God promised to Israel. The person who denies that Jesus is the Christ is an "antichrist" (one who opposes Christ).
- *Confess Christ has come in the flesh (4:1-3).* To deny that Jesus came in the flesh is to oppose the plain teaching of Scripture and to deny that a blood sacrifice was made for our sins.
- *Confess Jesus as the Son of God (4:14-15; 5:5-12).* One who confesses that Jesus is the Son of God has fellowship with God. God Himself has born witness that Jesus is His Son (Matthew 3:17; 17:5). To deny this truth makes God out to be a liar, which is a serious charge to make against God. He who acknowledges that Jesus is God's divine Son has access to eternal life (John 1:12). Maintaining the correct understanding of the person and nature of Jesus is essential for our salvation (1 John 5:13).

QUESTIONS

11. What does the word *Christ* mean? ____

____

____

12. Explain the consequences of denying that Jesus came in the flesh. ______

____

____

____

13. What blessings are available to the one who confesses that Jesus is the Son of God (4:15; 5:5, 11-12)? ______________________________

14. The one who denies that Jesus is the Son of God makes God out to be a ______________ (5:10).

15. Who is an antichrist (2:22; 4:3)? ______________________________

Those Who Do Not Practice Sin (3:4-10)

Since the Gnostics believed it was impossible for God to be associated with physical matter, they came to believe it was also impossible for their own spirits to be associated with physical matter. This was another false practice that grew out of the Gnostic error on the evil nature of physical matter. They claimed anything they did with their physical bodies did not affect their spirits. This provided a license to commit sin.

Some who called themselves Christians were ignoring God's laws and habitually engaging in sin. A person is known to be righteous by the way he lives his life, not because he claims to be a righteous person. The one who practices sin instead of righteousness is not of God.

QUESTIONS

16. How does John define sin (3:4; 5:17)? ______________________________

17. How does a person prove he is righteous (3:7)? ______________________________

18. List two things that characterize the children of the devil (3:10). ______________

SECOND JOHN

Recipients

"To the elect lady and her children" (v. 1). We do not know if this is a specific individual or a local congregation.

Purpose

To warn against receiving and aiding false teachers (vv. 9-11).

The teachings given by Christ and passed on by the apostles provide a barrier within which every Christian must live. The person who transgresses and does not abide in the teachings of Christ does not have fellowship with God. The Christian who extends fellowship to one who is out of fellowship with God destroys his own fellowship with God. Christians cannot have fellowship with those who are out of fellowship with God. We cannot recognize them as faithful Christians, encourage them in their spiritual efforts or aid them in these efforts.

THIRD JOHN

Recipients

Gaius (v. 1).

Purpose

To encourage Gaius in his service to the Lord.

Gaius was a man well known for his willingness to help and encourage other Christians. John commended him for this and encouraged him to continue.

John also spoke of a man named Diotrephes who wanted to be seen as a leader in the church. He spoke against the apostle John and his associates, refused to receive faithful brethren, and excommunicated those who went against his wishes. John would deal with him in person (vv. 9-10).

No individual Christian is allowed to "run" a local congregation of God's people. Jesus is the head of the church (Ephesians 1:22-23). A plurality of elders, not a single pastor or bishop, is appointed to oversee each local church (Acts 14:23; Titus 1:5; 1 Peter 5:1-4).

QUESTIONS

19. What does it mean to abide in the doctrine of Christ (2 John 9)? ________

20. What happens to the Christian who does not abide in the doctrine of Christ? ________

21. What happens to the Christian who extends fellowship to one who is not abiding in the doctrine of Christ (vv. 10-11)? ________

22. What brought the apostle John his greatest joy (3 John 4)? ________

23. What sins were being committed by Diotrephes (vv. 9-10)? ________

24. Can a local church have elders if only one man is qualified to serve? Why or why not? ________

Conclusion

Fellowship is a great blessing. Through Jesus Christ, the Christian has fellowship with God. We maintain this fellowship by walking in the light of God's commands. The Christian can also have fellowship with other Christians. This fellowship is maintained by love. However, the Christian must be careful not to extend fellowship to the wrong people or to deny fellowship to the right people.

Made in the USA
Columbia, SC
01 April 2025